The Layman's United States Constitution

The Product of Two Highly Trained
Enlisted Army Veterans with
Attitudes

Timothy Imholt Ph.D.
Michael Garst B.S.

The text used for the original sections of The Constitution of the United States was obtained from the National Archives. Their website can be found at:

www.archives.gov/exhibits/charters/constitution.html

Navigating to the portion labeled Read Transcript. This website has a great deal of information about the founding documents of the United States of America. Please read them before quoting them, don't just trust the nightly news to make sure the quotes are correct.

Questions concerning the rights of this book should be addressed to tim@timothyimholt.com.

TIM'S DEDICATION

This book is dedicated to my late father, Louis Walter Imholt. He loved every aspect of this country's founding and was a true patriot. He also had no place for people "lawyering" things as much as seems to happen currently. He also had very little patience for the modern crop of politicians. This book is a logical, understandable explanation of the US Constitution, what it means, and hopefully that can be achieved in such a way no one can guess my personal politics. I shall do my best Dad, I hope that this lives up to the standards you set for unbiased pursuit of facts.

MICHAEL'S DEDICTION

I want to dedicate this book to the wonderful support that I received from my family and friends. All who have stood by me in good times and not so good times. They are the ones, which make things like this not only possible but also, very important. With out them, none of this would have been possible. Besides, who would I be if I did not dedicate this work to those who have sacrificed so dearly for what this book contains? For all those who have risked so much, this is for you, and just as important, Thank you.

CONTENTS

Introduction

Oftentimes the books written about the documents that formed this Country are deep in either political points of view (slanted to one extreme wing of the political spectrum or the other) or, even worse, "lawyerspeak." This book represents our very best attempt to avoid either of those. In fact, it is our greatest hope that you will finish, having read this book, unable to guess which political party we typically associate ourselves with, if we associate with one at all.

Given the current state of the two major political parties in this country it is sometimes less stressful to not associate with either one. The largest challenge we see today in the political dialog that dominates the nightly news is that if you claim to be from one party people from the other party run quickly away to avoid any kind of discussion with you. This is for fear that someone inside their party will call them a RINO or DINO (Republican or Democrat In Name Only).

This not being able to come together problems we face really does need to end. The two major parties need to be able to, once again, come together and find ways to go through some amount of give and take to do what is best for the Nation, not what is best for their party. Sadly, all too often, decisions are made for what is best for a particular ideology or special interest instead of what is best for the

Citizenry.

You will find that in the discussion sections of each Article and Amendment we make some statements that are very likely to make the fringes of both major political parties...perturbed is probably as good a word as any. If we are extremely lucky, it is our deepest hope, that we will piss these fringes off in ways they haven't been pissed off in years. They do deserve this once in a while. We did stop short of saying anything our respective Drill Sergeants said to us over the time we both spent in various military training courses, but we did apply a dose of common sense and logic.

This book came to be because we realized, after talking to many people (including several sitting politicians), that there are some grotesque misinterpretations and general misquotes from the Constitution floating around the Internet centric world we live in. We felt that might, be at least in part, because people just didn't understand the document. The language is an older style, there have been loads of amendments, and it is relatively complex.

To add to that complexity are the facts that many of the attempts at interpretation of this document, appear to be done by people who didn't understand the language. We make that statement under the assumption that they chose to attempt to read the document before explaining it to others, something that might be in question with some of the so-called subject matter experts we see on television every night.

—

While doing research for this book we read several other books on this subject and examined many websites. There can be no finer example of the over the top interpretations that are running around about this document than in the one case we found in the form of an explanation to the Preamble that went on and on for thirty-eight pages.

Think about that. The Preamble to the Constitution is one sentence. Someone explained it for thirty-eight pages. It's a great sentence but, seriously, thirty-eight pages?

What is needed in this world is a quick, high-level, not condescending interpretation and discussion written for people who are not University Professors specializing in the Constitution. There needs to be a discussion, explanation, and understandable book for everyone else, who doesn't have time to read thirty eight pages about every single sentence, and yes that level of academic rigor does exist for this entire document if you have the time to read it.

Even as we wrote this, we cringed at the very thought of thirty-eight page explanations for any point let alone each point. There is a time and a place for that, but this book isn't it.

We aim to remove that complexity so we can all at least have the same starting point when we discuss our founding laws. The Constitution is the legal rulebook from which all other rules derive. We should, as a well-informed citizenry, understand the rulebook.

How do we accomplish this goal?

Well, it is simple. The first thing we have done is made every attempt to write a modern language version of every single Article and Amendment without changing any meaning to fulfill some hidden political agenda.

We have no agenda other than healthy kids, a healthy economy, and a country that can once again sit down and talk about problems with one another in a rational manner.

We are not offering up our modern day language versions of this document and saying the original should be replaced with a more modern document. We very much think the contrary is true. We should always refer to the original "owner's manual for the country" and only modify it through the normal amendment process, which will be discussed in this book. The Constitution is the rulebook for everything we do in this Country and we should not throw out a rulebook that has served us well for so many years. We must merely understand that rulebook a little better.

Who are we?

We are both Army Veterans (although we don't claim to speak for all Veterans), one of us (Michael) is a disabled Army Veteran. More importantly, we are American's who care about the future of everyone who lives in this country.

We don't just care about those who agree with us.

We don't just care about those who vote along the same party lines as us (assuming we vote along party lines, which may not be true).

We *do* care about all those who proudly call themselves Citizens of these United States.

This is book is written without over lawyering, don't worry that was easy; we aren't lawyers, as that linguistic style would surely be confusing, and alleviating confusion is what we are here for.

We want to stress a fact, neither of are lawyers. We have nothing against lawyers but we hope to be able to help people who don't spend everyday dealing with the laws of this Country to understand their foundation.

Back to the subject at hand. The original language of the document uses many terms that are just, simply, not used today.

Between us we, the former Enlisted Soldiers who wrote this book have three College Degrees. Each of us has a 4-year BS degree and one PhD. None of those degrees are in law. None of those degrees are in English. We are literally just two guys who want people to understand this document as fully as possible without having to spend hours with a thesaurus, or taking a college course. We did the hard work for you.

Then, finally, in each chapter, we will briefly attempt to explain what the words mean to us in an apolitical fashion. We do this final section without a political agenda, without trying to push a policy; we merely do it as what we are, veterans, a physicist, a manager, fathers, husbands and Americans. You will find that in these discussion sections we are very likely to make the political fringes of both parties angrier than a bargain-hunting shopper who missed

Black Friday sales.

With all of that in mind, we will start with the Preamble, but we promise not to go on for thirty-eight pages.

Our most sincere hope is that people will read this book and gain a better understanding of a Document that we should all understand but not everyone has the time to take a semester (or two) long University Course.

We will try to divide this book up into digestible chunks consumable in a single sitting.

Most of all, we hope that everyone who reads this will think about these words, and the Founders who fought a War to give us the Country we love.

We appreciate you giving us your time, and we hope we have honored those who gave us this great Nation.

Chapter 1

Preamble

Original Text of the Preamble of the Constitution of the United States

We the People of the United States, in Order to form a more perfect Union, establish Justice, insure domestic Tranquility, provide for the common defence, promote the general Welfare, and secure the Blessings of Liberty to ourselves and our Posterity, do ordain and establish this Constitution for the United States of America.

Modern Text of the Preamble of the Constitution of the United States

We the people of the United States deserve a more perfect Nation. In order achieve this goal we must establish Justice, insure domestic Peace, provide for the Nation's defense, and promote the general welfare. As part of this improved country we will secure the blessing of Independence. We must also guarantee these things for future generations. We will do these things in the newly formed United States of America.

Discussion

What do these words mean and why should we care?

How do they impact our lives and in what ways are they important today?

Why were these words, or even this section, included in the Constitution in the first place?

This opening was there so that the Founding Fathers could explain why they were forming a new government and abandoning the Articles of Confederation. They wanted to give an introduction to what was coming. Think of it like a preview of coming attractions, or perhaps a movie preview.

These men were sent to what became the Constitutional Convention to fix the Articles, not to write, or create a whole new form of Government. There was some...caution used in getting this information out, and the Founders chose to explain themselves right up front.

The Articles of Confederation were this Country's original form of Federal Government and they didn't work very well. With this newly formed government they hoped to achieve the goals they fought so hard for in the Revolutionary War. It was just that simple.

As an interesting side note, George Washington made everyone at the convention swear secrecy about what they were doing, even from their families. These men could have been guilty of Treason in their War against England (had they lost they certainly would have been found guilty of this and executed) and the decision to abandon one government and start a whole new one could have been considered Treason again. They were so concerned that there is an urban legend in Boston (where Tim lives, not where the Convention took place but Boston does love a good urban legend) that they sent people out with Benjamin Franklin at night (he liked beer) just to be sure he didn't drink too much and start to talk.

Franklin is often (incorrectly) quoted as having said, "Beer is proof God loves us and wants us to be happy." How we wish he really said that. What he really said was, "Behold the rain which descends from heaven upon our vineyards, there it enters the roots of the vines, to be changed into wine, a constant proof that God loves us, and loves to see us happy." Ben was a bit more verbose than the phrase that fits well on a t-shirt, but the sentiment is very real.

In this preamble they wanted to be absolutely sure that everyone knew that the rights of this new government did not just belong to a select few at the top, but truly belonged to everyone. It was important that they informed anyone who would listen that this government belonged to all citizens of this Country, and that they were all considered equal under the law (with some exceptions, that were later amended, to be discussed in this book).

Why would they specifically call out Justice?

One of the many reasons behind the War for Independence was a fair trial. It wasn't just about fair trade or even taxation without representation, like many things in life there was no one reason, it was also about Justice. A fair trial was not something a colonist was guaranteed. The Founders wanted to ensure that all citizens would be considered equal under the law (details on this later). This was important to these men, and should remain important to every one of us today.

What about the phrase Insure Domestic Tranquility?

At this point in our history there had been some uprisings. Most of those had been over things like a bad economy and repayment of war debts (Shay's Rebellion for instance).

There were likely going to be more of these types of things as the Confederation of States had, among other problems, a large amount of debt and no really effective way to raise funds. Think about it, they had a method to spend money but no real mechanism to raise funds (through taxation for instance or maybe a massive bake sale). They also had debt problems. Let's hope today's political leadership doesn't throw out our form of Government because of our current debt problems and take what we have said here as an "aha so that's how to do it." As we will see later in this book the Founders took on the debts accrued under the Articles of Confederation and made them the responsibility of the United States of American under the Constitution.

The Founders thought there would be a large number of these uprisings, as well as other problems that were becoming obvious, if something wasn't done. As a result they decided to throw away the Articles of Confederation and write The Constitution. The Articles had other issues as well, and this seemed to be the easier, and more effective, solution.

Due to all they had been through as a young Nation, they felt it was important to call out that one of the purposes of a federal government should be to keep peace within the Nation's borders in addition to protecting the outer borders. The Articles of Confederation were really lacking in this type of authority. Sure the States could defend themselves but, in the long run, would that be enough? Certainly it would not have been sufficient in the War against England.

When it comes to the common defense (spelled with the modern day "s" in the modernized text rather than the colonial period "c") the Founders knew that attacks within their borders by another country were a very real possibility. They had just fought a war here.

The statement about the general welfare can, and has, been interpreted in many different ways over the years.

In the time this document was written the Founders were pretty clear in other writings that they meant well being. They didn't mean anything more than that. In fact, many scholars have interpreted this to mean that if they did the previous three things they called out, Justice, Tranquility and Military this would be solved and well being would be taken care of by default.

While it is impossible to ask the Founders what they meant, if you go back and read other things that these same men wrote, it seems clear that they meant exactly what these scholars have said. That there was a minimum standard being set, that's it. We will also see that later in the document they wanted to be sure to set absolute upper limits on the powers of a Federal Government.

Think about that, they wanted to be sure that the Government could not grow in power until the people no longer had any amount of say-so and the government had it all. Something we should try to keep in mind every time there is a new department added to the mix in Washington (such as Homeland Security which we aren't saying is bad just should be watched).

Back to our point, they wanted a guarantee of well being or put another way, safety. That was the extent of their intention under the Constitution. It did not prohibit further action; it merely set a minimum standard to be achieved. We can argue over what that minimum standard should be, and we can do additional things over and above that minimum, but the only Constitutionally guaranteed right is that minimum standard.

This Nation, according to our Constitution, does not owe anyone a living; it merely owes them the opportunity to earn one free of the issues that would arise from a lack of Justice, Domestic Tranquility, and Common Defense. It seems clear that was the original intent. The Founders were charitable men, and as a people, Americans are charitable, but as far as governmental responsibility these three things were the minimum of the day.

The final statement in the preamble with the phrase "secure the Blessings of Liberty to ourselves and our Posterity" is very important.

These same men had fought a very long, very hard war with England. They did so because England kept passing unjust laws, and in many ways abusing the Colonists good will. They wanted to be sure that this new Federal Government, while insuring these other rights, could not oppress the citizens in other ways.

The document itself was aimed at attempting to make sure that what they had just done in that War wasn't going to become necessary again.

They had to throw off one government and form another. They wanted to be sure that this new government could not be guilty of the same oppressive behavior that England had been guilty of.

The Preamble serves as an introduction to the rest of the document while not being a law of any kind. It merely outlines what the rest of the document will fill in the details of.

That outline is the form of government we live under today, a Republic.

Chapter 2

Article I

Article I of the Constitution of the United States lays out the structure, as well as the powers of the Congress. It has ten sections and we will go through them one at a time with the original followed by a section containing the more modern version of the text. This breakdown, we feel, makes it easier to digest and, ultimately, understand. The discussion will be held for the end of the Article.

Original Text of Article I Section I the Constitution of the United States

All legislative Powers herein granted shall be vested in a Congress of the United States, which shall consist of a Senate and House of Representatives.

Modern Text of Article I Section I of the Constitution of the United States

All of the lawmaking powers allowed in this government are assigned to the Congress of the United States. The Congress will be broken down into two sections, or Houses, named the Senate and the House of Representatives.

Original Text of Article I Section II the Constitution of the United States

The House of Representatives shall be composed of Members chosen every second Year by the People of the several States, and the Electors in each State shall have the Qualifications requisite for Electors of the most numerous Branch of the State Legislature.

No Person shall be a Representative who shall not have attained to the Age of twenty five Years, and been seven Years a Citizen of the United States, and who shall not, when elected, be an Inhabitant of that State in which he shall be chosen.

Representatives and direct Taxes shall be apportioned among the several States which may be included within this Union, according to their respective Numbers, which shall be determined by adding to the whole Number of free Persons, including those bound to Service for a Term of Years, and excluding Indians not taxed, three fifths of all other Persons. The actual Enumeration shall be made within three Years after the first Meeting of the Congress of the United States, and within every subsequent Term of ten Years, in such Manner as they shall by Law direct. The Number of Representatives shall not exceed one for every thirty Thousand, but each State shall have at Least one Representative; and until such enumeration shall be made, the State of New Hampshire shall be entitled to chuse three, Massachusetts eight, Rhode-Island and Providence Plantations one, Connecticut five, New-York six, New Jersey four, Pennsylvania eight, Delaware one, Maryland six, Virginia ten, North Carolina five, South Carolina five, and Georgia three.

When vacancies happen in the Representation from any State, the Executive Authority thereof shall issue Writs of Election to fill such Vacancies.

The House of Representatives shall chuse their Speaker and other Officers; and shall have the sole Power of Impeachment.

Modern Text of Article I Section II of the Constitution of the United States

The portion of the Congress known as the House of Representatives will be made up of membership with people chosen from every state in the Union. These members will be elected every two years.

In order to be a member of the United States House of Representatives (the lower house of Congress) an individual must be twenty-five years of age. The membership of this House must also have been a citizen of the United States for seven years and, when elected, live in the State he or she was elected to represent.

Representatives and taxes will be assigned to the States of the Union in proportion to their population.

The population of the States will be determined by adding up the number of free people, including those bound to service for some period of time. These populations will also exclude Indians, who will not be taxed, as well as three fifths of all other people (slaves).

The population of the States will be determined by conducting a census. The first census will be made within three years of the first meeting of the Congress of the United States and every ten years after that. This shall be done in a method that will be described by law.

The number of representatives that each state gets

will not exceed one for every thirty thousand residents. Each State, regardless of population, will get at least one Representative.

Until a census can be achieved the State of New Hampshire will receive three, Massachusetts eight, Rhode Island and Providence Plantations one, Connecticut five, New York six, New Jersey four, Pennsylvania eight, Delaware one, Maryland six, Virginia ten, North Carolina five, South Carolina five and George three.

When a vacancy occurs (e.g. a representative resigns, is impeached or passes away) the Executive Authority (e.g. Governor) of the State who has lost a Representative shall issue a Writ of Election and fill the vacancy. This will cause a special election to be held, out of the normal election cycle, to allow the people of that State to choose a new Representative.

The House of Representatives will have the power to fill their leadership roles (e.g. Speaker of the House and other Officer positions). They shall also have the sole power of Impeachment.

Original Text of Article I Section III of the Constitution of the United States

The Senate of the United States shall be composed of two Senators from each State, chosen by the Legislature thereof for six Years; and each Senator shall have one Vote.

Immediately after they shall be assembled in Consequence of the first Election, they shall be divided as equally as may be into three Classes. The Seats of the Senators of the first Class shall be vacated at the Expiration of the second Year, of the second Class at the Expiration of the fourth Year, and of the third Class at the Expiration of the sixth Year, so that one third may be chosen every second Year; and if Vacancies happen by Resignation, or otherwise, during the Recess of the Legislature of any State, the Executive thereof may make temporary Appointments until the next Meeting of the Legislature, which shall then fill such Vacancies.

No Person shall be a Senator who shall not have attained to the Age of thirty Years, and been nine Years a Citizen of the United States, and who shall not, when elected, be an Inhabitant of that State for which he shall be chosen.

The Vice President of the United States shall be President of the Senate, but shall have no Vote, unless they be equally divided.

The Senate shall chuse their other Officers, and also a President pro tempore, in the Absence of the Vice President, or when he shall exercise the Office of President of the United States.

The Senate shall have the sole Power to try all Impeachments. When sitting for that Purpose, they shall be on Oath or Affirmation. When the President of the United States is tried, the Chief Justice shall preside: And no Person shall be convicted without the Concurrence of two thirds of the Members present.

Judgment in Cases of Impeachment shall not extend further than to removal from Office, and disqualification to hold and enjoy any Office of honor, Trust or Profit under the United States: but the Party convicted shall nevertheless be liable and subject to Indictment, Trial, Judgment and Punishment, according to Law.

Modern Text of Article I Section III of the Constitution of the United States

The Senate of the United States will be the Upper House of the Congress. This Legislative Body shall be made up of two Senators from each State. These Senators will not be chosen by the people but will be chosen by the Legislatures of each of the States. Each Senator will serve for a period of six years and get one vote.

Once the first Senate has been elected they will be divided into three equal groups. The seats of the first group will be vacated at the end of the second year, the second group will be vacated at the end of the fourth year, and the third group will be vacated at the end of the sixth year. As a result, one third of the Senate will be elected every second year. If vacancies occur as a result of resignation, or some other reason, while the Legislature of that State is on recess, the Executive of that State will fill those vacancies.

In order to serve as a Senator a person must be thirty-five years old, and have been a Citizen of the United States for at least nine years. They must also be a resident of the State they were elected to represent.

The Vice President of the United States is the President of the Senate. Despite this he does not vote on any legislation unless there is a tie amongst the Senators. In that instance it is the Vice President who casts the tie-breaking vote.

Other than the Vice President, the Senators shall choose their own officers, as well as a President pro tempore. The President pro tempore will be the person who acts in place of the Senate President when he is not available, for instance (but not limited to) when the Vice President had to take the office of President and no new Vice President has taken office.

The Senate is the only place where an impeachment trial (e.g. punishment phase of the impeachment proceedings) will take place. When they meet for this purpose they shall do so only after taking an oath swearing to tell the truth. In the case of the impeachment of the President of the United States, the Chief Justice of the Supreme Court shall preside over the proceedings. No punishment from these trials shall be considered agreed upon unless two thirds of the Members vote yes.

In the case of an impeachment the punishment shall not be anything greater than removal from office, and disqualification to hold official office in the United States again. If a person is impeached they can be held liable for crimes committed and put on trial in a criminal court according to the law.

Original Text of Article I Section IV of the Constitution of the United States

The Times, Places and Manner of holding Elections for Senators and Representatives, shall be prescribed in each State by the Legislature thereof; but the Congress may at any time by Law make or alter such Regulations, except as to the Places of chusing Senators.

The Congress shall assemble at least once in every

Year, and such Meeting shall be on the first Monday in December, unless they shall by Law appoint a different Day.

Modern Text of Article I Section IV of the Constitution of the United States

The times, locations, and methods of holding elections for Senators and other Representatives will be determined by each of the States. However, Congress may, at any time, pass a law to alter the regulations put forward by the States with the exception of the location of the vote. The State can always determine the location of the vote.

Congress shall meet at least once every year. The first day of that meeting will be the first Monday in December unless a law has been passed that appoints a different day.

Original Text of Article I Section V of the Constitution of the United States

Each House shall be the Judge of the Elections, Returns and Qualifications of its own Members, and a Majority of each shall constitute a Quorum to do Business; but a smaller Number may adjourn from day to day, and may be authorized to compel the Attendance of absent Members, in such Manner, and under such Penalties as each House may provide.

Each House may determine the Rules of its Proceedings, punish its Members for disorderly Behaviour, and, with the Concurrence of two thirds, expel a Member.

Each House shall keep a Journal of its Proceedings, and from time to time publish the same, excepting such Parts as may in their Judgment require Secrecy; and the Yeas and Nays of the Members of either House on any question shall, at the Desire of one fifth of those Present, be entered on the Journal.

Neither House, during the Session of Congress, shall, without the Consent of the other, adjourn for more than three days, nor to any other Place than that in which the two Houses shall be sitting.

Modern Text of Article I Section V of the Constitution of the United States

Each House in the Congress shall be able to determine if its members were justly elected and also be able to determine if they meet the Constitutional qualifications for the appropriate office.

In order to conduct business within either House a majority of members must be present and that majority will constitute what is called a Quorum. A number smaller than a quorum may adjourn from day to day, and that same smaller number is allowed to force additional members to attend in order to reach a quorum. If additional members refuse to attend, the two houses may impose whatever penalties they decide are appropriate.

The two Houses can write their own rules for their proceedings. They may also determine punishments for their own membership's disorderly behavior, should any occur. They may also, if two thirds of the membership agrees, expel, or dismiss a member.

Each House of Congress must keep notes of their proceedings. From time to time they must publish those notes, except for the portions they determine require secrecy, for example in the case of National Security. If one fifth of the members present agree, the voting record (yeas and nays) of the membership on any or all legislative votes shall be part of those notes.

If Congress is in session neither House is allowed to adjourn without the consent of the other for more than three days. Additionally, neither house may meet at a location separate from the other.

Original Text of Article I Section VI of the Constitution of the United States

The Senators and Representatives shall receive a Compensation for their Services, to be ascertained by Law, and paid out of the Treasury of the United States. They shall in all Cases, except Treason, Felony and Breach of the Peace, be privileged from Arrest during their Attendance at the Session of their respective Houses, and in going to and returning from the same; and for any Speech or Debate in either House, they shall not be questioned in any other Place.

No Senator or Representative shall, during the Time for which he was elected, be appointed to any civil Office under the Authority of the United States, which shall have been created, or the Emoluments whereof shall have been encreased during such time; and no Person holding any Office under the United States, shall be a Member of either House during his Continuance in Office.

Modern Text of Article I Section VI of the Constitution of the United States

The Senators and Representatives will receive a salary for their services. The amount of that salary will be written into law and paid from the Treasury of the United States.

With the exception of treason, felony, and breach of peace members will not be arrested during their attendance at the meeting of their respective Houses. Members are not to be arrested for any reason, other than those listed, while traveling to and from those meetings for speeches or debates in either House. They are not to be questioned for crimes in any other place other than in their elected House.

No Senator or Representative, while serving in his or her elected office, shall be appointed to any civil office under the authority of the United States for which a salary is received. No person holding such a civil office, who is then elected to either the Senate or the House of Representatives, shall continue to hold that civil office while holding the elected office.

Original Text of Article I Section VII of the Constitution of the United States

All Bills for raising Revenue shall originate in the House of Representatives; but the Senate may propose or concur with Amendments as on other Bills.

Every Bill which shall have passed the House of Representatives and the Senate, shall, before it become a Law, be presented to the President of the United States: If he approve he shall sign it, but if not he shall return it, with his Objections to that House in which it shall have originated, who shall enter the Objections at large on their Journal, and proceed to reconsider it. If after such Reconsideration two thirds of that House shall agree to pass the Bill, it shall be sent, together with the Objections, to the other House, by which it shall likewise be reconsidered, and if approved by two thirds of that House, it shall become a Law. But in all such Cases the Votes of both Houses shall be determined by yeas and Nays, and the Names of the Persons voting for and against the Bill shall be entered on the Journal of each House respectively. If any Bill shall not be returned by the President within ten Days (Sundays excepted) after it shall have been presented to him, the Same shall be a Law, in like Manner as if he had signed it, unless the Congress by their Adjournment prevent its Return, in which Case it shall not be a Law.

Every Order, Resolution, or Vote to which the Concurrence of the Senate and House of Representatives may be necessary (except on a question of Adjournment) shall be presented to the President of the United States; and before the Same shall take Effect, shall be approved by him, or being disapproved by him, shall be repassed by two thirds of the Senate and House of Representatives, according to the Rules and Limitations prescribed in the Case of a Bill.

Modern Text of Article I Section VII of the Constitution of the United States

All laws involving the collection of a tax shall start in the House of Representatives. The Senate may propose amendments in the same fashion they do on other Bills.

Every Bill that passes the House of Representatives

and the Senate must be presented to the President of the United States. If the President approves of the Bill he can sign it, and then it is enacted into law. If he does not approve of it he can return it, with his objections to the House that originated it. The Legislature must enter the President's objections into their Journal and proceed to reconsider the Bill.

If, after reconsideration, two thirds of that House agrees to pass the Bill, it shall be sent along with the President's objections to the other House. If the other House passes it with two thirds of their members agreeing, it shall become law. In all such cases the votes of both Houses will be determined by voting yes or no and the Names of the representatives voting for and against the Bill will be entered into the Journal of the respective House.

If the President does not return a Bill within ten days (not counting Sundays) after it was presented to him or her, the Bill shall become a Law, just as if it had been signed. This time period is only effective in the cases when Congress is in session. If the Congress sends the President a Bill and within ten days adjourns to prevent the Bill's return, the Bill will not become law.

Every order, resolution or vote that the Senate and House of Representatives agrees upon (except the motion to adjourn) shall be presented to the President of the United States. Before that order, resolution, or vote can take effect it shall be approved or disapproved by the President. If it is disapproved by the President it will only be enacted after it passes by the two thirds majority of the Senate and House of

Representatives according to the rules and limitations prescribed in this section of the Constitution.

Original Text of Article I Section VIII of the Constitution of the United States

The Congress shall have Power To lay and collect Taxes, Duties, Imposts and Excises, to pay the Debts and provide for the common Defence and general Welfare of the United States; but all Duties, Imposts and Excises shall be uniform throughout the United States;

To borrow Money on the credit of the United States;

To regulate Commerce with foreign Nations, and among the several States, and with the Indian Tribes;

To establish an uniform Rule of Naturalization, and uniform Laws on the subject of Bankruptcies throughout the United States;

To coin Money, regulate the Value thereof, and of foreign Coin, and fix the Standard of Weights and Measures;

To provide for the Punishment of counterfeiting the Securities and current Coin of the United States;

To establish Post Offices and post Roads;

To promote the Progress of Science and useful Arts, by securing for limited Times to Authors and Inventors the exclusive Right to their respective Writings and Discoveries;

To constitute Tribunals inferior to the supreme Court;

To define and punish Piracies and Felonies committed on the high Seas, and Offences against the Law of Nations;

To declare War, grant Letters of Marque and Reprisal, and make Rules concerning Captures on Land and Water;

To raise and support Armies, but no Appropriation of Money to that Use shall be for a longer Term than two Years;

To provide and maintain a Navy;

To make Rules for the Government and Regulation of the land and naval Forces;

To provide for calling forth the Militia to execute the Laws of the Union, suppress Insurrections and repel Invasions;

To provide for organizing, arming, and disciplining, the Militia, and for governing such Part of them as may be employed in the Service of the United States, reserving to the States respectively, the Appointment of the Officers, and the Authority of training the Militia according to the discipline prescribed by Congress;

To exercise exclusive Legislation in all Cases whatsoever, over such District (not exceeding ten Miles square) as may, by Cession of particular States, and the Acceptance of Congress, become the Seat of the Government of the United States, and to exercise like Authority over all Places purchased by the Consent of the Legislature of the State in which the Same shall be, for the Erection of Forts, Magazines, Arsenals, dock-Yards, and other needful Buildings;--

And

To make all Laws which shall be necessary and proper for carrying into Execution the foregoing Powers, and all other Powers vested by this Constitution in the Government of the United States, or in any Department or Officer thereof.

Modern Text of Article I Section VIII of the Constitution of the United States

The Congress has the power to enact and collect taxes, duties, or excises. This is done in order to pay debts, provide for the common defense, as well as the general welfare of the United States. All of these Federal taxes, duties and excises must be uniform throughout the United States.

The Congress has the power to borrow money using the credit of the United States.

The Congress has the power to regulate commerce with foreign Nations, and among the States as well as with the Indian Tribes.

The Congress has the power to establish a uniform Rule of Naturalization, and uniform laws on the subject of Bankruptcies throughout the United States.

The Congress has the power to coin money, as well as regulate its value. They are also to fix the standard of weights and measures of that money.

The Congress has the power to pass punishments for the counterfeiting of Securities and current Coin of the United States.

The Congress has the power to establish a post office and post roads.

The Congress has the power to promote the progress of Science and useful Arts. This is done by securing, for limited times, the rights to authors and inventors the rights to their writings and discoveries in the form of copyrights and patents.

The Congress has the power to confirm judges in Courts lower than the Supreme Court.

The Congress has the power to punish piracies and felonies committed on the high Seas as well as offenses against the Law of Nations.

The Congress has the power to declare War, grant letters of retaliation against an enemy and to make rules concerning the capture of enemy combatants upon the land and water during times of conflict.

The Congress has the power to raise and support Armies, however no appropriation of money for this use will be valid for more than two years.

The Congress has the power to build and maintain a Navy.

The Congress has the power to make rules for the governance and regulations of the Land and Naval Armed Forces.

The Congress has the power to provide for calling up the militia to execute the Laws of the Union, as well as to suppress revolt and repel an invasion.

The Congress has the power to provide for the organization, arming and disciplining of the militia as well as governing that part of the militia that is employed in the service of the Federal Government of the United States of America. The Congress shall reserve to the States the appointment of Officers and the authority to train the militia according to the discipline put forward by the Congress.

The Congress has the power to exercise exclusive legislation in all cases over the Nation's Capital. This power to exclusive legislation also pertains to all lands purchased by the consent of legislature for the building of forts, magazines, arsenals, dockyards and other needed federal buildings.

The Congress has the power to make all the laws necessary and proper for carrying into execution the powers listed in, and all other powers entrusted by this Constitution in the Government of the United States or any Department or Office it enacts into existence.

Original Text of Article I Section IX of the Constitution of the United States

The Migration or Importation of such Persons as any of the States now existing shall think proper to admit, shall not be prohibited by the Congress prior to the Year one thousand eight hundred and eight, but a Tax or duty may be imposed on such Importation, not exceeding ten dollars for each Person.

The Privilege of the Writ of Habeas Corpus shall not be suspended, unless when in Cases of Rebellion or Invasion the public Safety may require it.

No Bill of Attainder or ex post facto Law shall be passed.

No Capitation, or other direct, Tax shall be laid, unless in Proportion to the Census or enumeration herein before directed to be taken.

No Tax or Duty shall be laid on Articles exported from any State.

No Preference shall be given by any Regulation of Commerce or Revenue to the Ports of one State over those of another; nor shall Vessels bound to, or from, one State, be obliged to enter, clear, or pay Duties in another.

No Money shall be drawn from the Treasury, but in Consequence of Appropriations made by Law; and a regular Statement and Account of the Receipts and Expenditures of all public Money shall be published from time to time.

No Title of Nobility shall be granted by the United States: And no Person holding any Office of Profit or Trust under them, shall, without the Consent of the Congress, accept of any present, Emolument, Office, or Title, of any kind whatever, from any King, Prince, or foreign State.

Modern Text of Article I Section IX of the Constitution of the United States

The immigration of people coming into the United States shall not be prohibited by the Congress prior to the year one thousand eight hundred and eight; however Congress may decide to collect a tax on immigrants during that time, not to exceed ten dollars per person.

The right of a citizen to appear before a judge shall not be suspended, except in the case of rebellion or invasion when the public safety may require otherwise.

A law passed after a citizen has performed an act that would break that new law has no relevance to the act committed.

No tax can be charged for the right to vote.

No tax can be charged on goods or services exported from one State and imported to another.

No regulation of commerce shall be passed that gives preference to a port of one State over another. Transportation bound to one state shall not be obligated to pay taxes upon entrance to another state.

No money shall be taken from the Treasury of the United States except when a law is passed directing the expenditure. A regular statement and accounting of the receipts and expenditures of all public money shall be published from time to time.

No title of Nobility will be granted by the United States. No person holding any office that is salaried by the government will take a gift, office, or title from a king, prince or foreign state without the permission of Congress.

Original Text of Article I Section X of the Constitution of the United States

No State shall enter into any Treaty, Alliance, or Confederation; grant Letters of Marque and Reprisal; coin Money; emit Bills of Credit; make any Thing but gold and silver Coin a Tender in Payment of Debts; pass any Bill of Attainder, ex post facto Law, or Law impairing the Obligation of Contracts, or grant any Title of Nobility.

No State shall, without the Consent of the Congress,

lay any Imposts or Duties on Imports or Exports, except what may be absolutely necessary for executing it's inspection Laws: and the net Produce of all Duties and Imposts, laid by any State on Imports or Exports, shall be for the Use of the Treasury of the United States; and all such Laws shall be subject to the Revision and Controul of the Congress.

No State shall, without the Consent of Congress, lay any Duty of Tonnage, keep Troops, or Ships of War in time of Peace, enter into any Agreement or Compact with another State, or with a foreign Power, or engage in War, unless actually invaded, or in such imminent Danger as will not admit of delay.

Modern Text of Article I Section X of the Constitution of the United States

No State can enter into a treaty, alliance or Confederation.

No State may grant letters of retaliation against an enemy.

No State shall coin money.

No State shall make anything but gold and silver coin money for payment of debts.

No State shall pass a Bill that infringes on a person's civil rights.

No State shall pass a law that causes infractions of the past to be in violation of that law.

No State shall pass a law imparting the obligation of contracts or grant the Title of Nobility to any person.

No State shall, without the consent of the Congress, tax any imports or exports, except what may be absolutely necessary for executing its inspection laws.

The net product of taxes by any State on imports or exports shall be for the use of the Treasury of the United States; and all such laws shall be subject to the revision as well as control of the Congress.

No State shall, without the consent of Congress, engage in War with another State or foreign power unless actually invaded or under such imminent danger that delay would cause harm to their citizens.

Discussion

This Article is all about the Congress. It is broken down into ten sections, which we will briefly discuss.

Section one of Article one is usually called the vesting clause. This is where the Congress is given the power to make the laws we are bound to live under. This is, essentially, their main purpose. They have only a few other tasks they are even permitted to do, and those will be discussed later in this chapter.

It was thought at the time the Constitution was written that giving a large group of people the responsibility of making the laws, rather than putting this in the hands of one person, such as a King, would make these laws much more representative of the people's will. This power residing in the Congress means that no other branch may execute this task and attempt to make a law.

There is always someone on the news talking about

how this President or that President are trying to use Executive Orders to "write law" or "get around" Congress. The interesting bit about Executive Orders is that they do not hold the same status as law. They might say that the President wants something done but people are under no obligation of the law to do so. I am sure that someone somewhere thinks we are pointing fingers at one particular President. We are not; recent Presidents all use this trick. It gets them on the news, and in some cases things even happen, but they shouldn't. The Congress does have mechanisms to stop this sort of behavior if they choose to do so. If these orders are really things they disagree with rather than finding the nearest television camera perhaps they should utilize those Constitutional mechanisms and put a stop to this sort of thing. That is their job. Checks and balances are real, and matter.

We also find out that the Congress will be broken into two Houses. The idea with this bicameral legislature was so that the whims of political winds blowing one way or another will be less influential than if we had a single House re-elected every two years. In other words one House was designed to give a type of adult supervision to the other. That might be our little not so subtle way of saying that at least one of the Houses has from time to time acted like children who didn't get their way, and that was completely intentional.

We doubt that the Founders anticipated the longevity of service we are currently faced with in some elected officials. Some of their writing spoke eloquently of citizen leadership. In other words people holding these offices were meant to have other jobs, other careers. These offices, we believe, were not meant to be lifetime positions.

There is an argument someone will state after reading this that says experience in a legislator matters. That is certainly true. However, in our opinion, so does life experience outside of the government. How the hell can someone be expected to set rules, regulations, and laws that better the lives of Americans if they are completely disconnected from the challenges faced by many of us.

Let's play out the experience question, versus the disconnected from the populace concept. There was a case of one Senator who was in elected office for an insane period of time. Strom Thurmond was first elected to public office in 1933. How long is reasonable for someone to serve? Twenty years? Thirty? He was in office until 2003. In this case he was in various elected offices for seven decades. Is that too much to be able to claim to understand those who are being represented? Well, that, of course, depends on the representative but it is something we should at least talk about. Should people be allowed to hold office that long? Let's have that public debate.

Section two tells us all about the House of Representatives. It is here that we learn that every member of this legislative body is elected every two years. We also find out that these Representatives are voted for by the citizenry in a direct democratic vote. The person with the most votes wins the election and is then the Representative for that

Congressional District.

Section three explains the Senate. It tells us that there are two Senators from each state, and they will serve six-year terms. We also learn something else interesting. That 1/3 of the Senate will be up for election every 2 years.

The Founders thought that this would give some continuity to the government. With the entire House of Representatives being up for election every two years, in theory, the entire body could be comprised of new members. They wanted some guarantee there would be some experienced hands in the Legislature and these rotating elections for the Senate, it was thought, would provide that.

Section four explains some unique rules concerning the Senate. It tells that the Senate has the power to determine when and how the elections will be held to elect members to the Senate and the House of Representatives. This section also adds that the Congress *must* meet at least once each year. In this rather unique section it basically lays out the rules for electing the Congress and the frequency they are required to meet.

It has been said by some that this section implies that we don't really need a full time Congress such as we have today. That may be their implication but they do not rule it out, they leave it up to the people to determine.

Although, if Tim had a vote in this matter he would want Congress to work as few days as possible. He would further request that Congress got paid as little as possible and was forced to keep other employment. Serving in these offices should be a privilege not something used as a one-way street to eternal wealth and privilege. At the time of this writing the salary of a Congressperson was $174,000. The average salary of an ex-Congressperson was nearly $2,000,000. Interestingly people still want to be re-elected, and many of them become very wealthy while serving in these offices. There are some questions that arise concerning these facts and how they accumulate that wealth while being a public servant, those questions need to be discussed publicly and often.

If Mike had a say in this section, there would also be term limits for each person elected into office. No one, absolutely no one should hold any office in the Congress for more than 2 terms. None of this being in office for 30, 40, 50 or even 60 years crap. Part of the reasoning for the rotation of election was to always keep new members in office with fresh ideas and a certain level of energy to help fuel the grand ideals of this great country.

Section five dives into procedures for each House of Congress. This is how they do business. This also includes the qualifications of the Representatives and Senators, as well as how to determine what rules they must follow.

Interestingly, the Founders felt it necessary to describe how records must be kept for what happens as well as how a house can adjourn a session. These are important things to organize or the two Houses may end up trying to do business differently than one another, leading to confusion. This section puts forward the method for the Congress to do business that ensures the Legislative Branch won't become a chaotic body (despite the way it appears on the nightly news) that does not have a reasonable method to do business.

Section six describes the privileges, restrictions and compensation for members of Congress. It says that the people in these offices get a salary.

It also says something that is not as widely known, and it should be in the modern world. These elected officials can't be arrested except for a felony, treason or breach of peace. In some ways this is a good thing, however, it has certainly led to some abuses over the years. This section also says that no one employed in one of these offices can take an office in the Executive Branch (e.g. President or Vice President) while they are still in Congress.

Section seven explains how Congress can make Laws. A bill can originate in either the House of Representatives or the Senate and once passed by both Houses goes to the President for his signature or veto. This is a very important section because it outlines how the Legislative Branch can override a Presidential veto, which is a very important way to balance out a President who may be trying to overcome the will of the people.

Section eight is probably the easiest section of this article to understand. It gives the enumerated powers of the Congress. It is a list of things that the Congress is specifically permitted to do.

Section nine is the limits of Congress. This is also important because is sets what the Congress can't do.

Without some of these being written into the Constitution it is clear that abuses of Power would be very possible and most likely would occur. Some Congressional sessions have certainly tested these limits but we have mechanisms to stop those power grabs. Checks and balances is a term commonly used and the other two branches of the Federal Government can put a stop to a power grab by any one branch.

Section ten was put in place to limit the Powers of the States. It says that if the federal government is given a power under the Constitution the States no longer will have that power (for example State's can't declare War on another Country). Think of it as a way to avoid confusion. Imagine what would happen if Texas (or any of the other 49 States) decided to declare War on another Country. Would the Federal Government be required to lend assistance? Would they be neutral? Those are hard to answer and some things should be left to the Federal Government and other things to the States.

Chapter 3
Article II

Article II of the Constitution of the United States lays out the structure, and the powers of the Executive Branch, or Presidency. In many ways the Founders were very specific in this section. They had just been through the Revolutionary War in which they had achieved freedom from a King; in the eyes of many that King was the head of what they viewed as a tyrannical Monarchy. They did not want to build a new Monarchy in their young Nation.

Original Text of Article II Section I the Constitution of the United States

The executive Power shall be vested in a President of the United States of America. He shall hold his Office during the Term of four Years, and, together with the Vice President, chosen for the same Term, be elected, as follows:

Each State shall appoint, in such Manner as the Legislature thereof may direct, a Number of Electors, equal to the whole Number of Senators and Representatives to which the State may be entitled in the Congress: but no Senator or Representative, or Person holding an Office of Trust or Profit under the United States, shall be appointed an Elector.

The Electors shall meet in their respective States, and vote by Ballot for two Persons, of whom one at least shall not be an Inhabitant of the same State with themselves. And they shall make a List of all the Persons voted for, and of the Number of Votes for each; which List they shall sign and certify, and transmit sealed to the Seat of the Government of the United States, directed to the President of the Senate. The President of the Senate shall, in the Presence of the Senate and House of Representatives, open all the Certificates, and the Votes shall then be counted. The Person having the greatest Number of Votes shall be the President, if such Number be a Majority of the whole Number of Electors appointed; and if there be more than one who have such Majority, and have an equal Number of Votes, then the House of Representatives shall immediately chuse by Ballot one of them for President; and if no Person have a Majority, then from the five highest on the List the said House shall in like Manner chuse the President. But in chusing the President, the Votes shall be taken by States, the Representation from each State having one Vote; A quorum for this purpose shall consist of a Member or Members from two thirds of the States, and a Majority of all the States shall be necessary to a Choice. In every Case, after the Choice of the President, the Person having the greatest Number of Votes of the Electors shall be the Vice President. But if there should remain two or more who have equal Votes, the Senate shall chuse from them by Ballot the Vice President.

The Congress may determine the Time of chusing the Electors, and the Day on which they shall give their Votes; which Day shall be the same throughout the United States.

No Person except a natural born Citizen, or a Citizen of the United States, at the time of the Adoption of this Constitution, shall be eligible to the Office of President; neither shall any Person be eligible to that Office who shall not have attained to the Age of thirty five Years, and been fourteen Years a Resident within the United States.

In Case of the Removal of the President from Office, or of his Death, Resignation, or Inability to discharge the Powers and Duties of the said Office, the Same shall devolve on the Vice President, and the Congress may by Law provide for the Case of Removal, Death, Resignation or Inability, both of the President and Vice President, declaring what Officer shall then act as President, and such Officer shall act accordingly, until the Disability be removed, or a President shall be elected.

The President shall, at stated Times, receive for his Services, a Compensation, which shall neither be increased nor diminished during the Period for which he shall have been elected, and he shall not receive within that Period any other Emolument from the United States, or any of them.

Before he enter on the Execution of his Office, he shall take the following Oath or Affirmation:--"I do solemnly swear (or affirm) that I will faithfully execute the Office of President of the United States, and will to the best of my Ability, preserve, protect and defend the Constitution of the United States."

Modern Text of Article II Section I the Constitution of the United States

Executive authority will be given to the President and Vice President of the United States of America. They will have a term of four years and will be selected at the same time.

Their election will occur in the following fashion:

Each of the states will choose, in any way the law sees fit, a number of electors equal to the number of Representatives and Senators each State has in the Congress. A Senator, Representative or anyone holding a position of power and authority in the United States Government cannot be selected as an Elector.

Each Elector will meet in their state and vote for two people by ballot. One of those two people cannot reside in their own state. The electors will make a list of all people voted for and the number of votes received, then send the results in a sealed manner with the transcription signed and certified with the names of each elector and vote tallies to the President of the Senate.

The President of the Senate will open each transcription in front of the Senate and count each person and the number of votes. The person with the highest votes becomes the President of the United States. If there is not a majority winner, or a tie, the House of Representatives will choose a winner. The person with the second highest votes becomes the Vice President of the United States.

The body of Congress will set a date and a time for the Electors to place their votes. This date and time will be the same across the entire United States.

Only a person who is born a citizen of the United States or has become a Naturalized Citizen of the United States at the time this document is accepted can become the President. Anyone who would become the President would have to be at least thirty five years old and have been a resident of the United States for the previous fourteen years.

If the office of the President is vacated due to death, mental illness, resignation, or legal removal, the Vice President shall take over the authority of the Presidency. Congress may, if the situation demands it, name a person to stand as President until either a new President is elected or the current President has overcome his disability.

The President and Vice President will receive a salary for their service. This salary will be the same amount the entire time they serve as the President or Vice President. They will not receive any other payment from the government.

Before the newly elected President takes his place in office, he must swear an oath stating that he will "Faithfully execute the duties of the Office of the President of the United States to the best of his ability and protect and defend the Constitution of the United States."

Original Text of Article II Section II the Constitution of the United States

The President shall be Commander in Chief of the Army and Navy of the United States, and of the Militia of the several States, when called into the actual Service of the United States; he may require the Opinion, in writing, of the principal Officer in each of the executive Departments, upon any Subject relating to the Duties of their respective Offices, and he shall have Power to grant Reprieves and Pardons for Offences against the United States, except in Cases of Impeachment.

He shall have Power, by and with the Advice and Consent of the Senate, to make Treaties, provided two thirds of the Senators present concur; and he shall nominate, and by and with the Advice and Consent of the Senate, shall appoint Ambassadors, other public Ministers and Consuls, Judges of the supreme Court, and all other Officers of the United States, whose Appointments are not herein otherwise provided for, and which shall be established by Law: but the Congress may by Law vest the Appointment of such inferior Officers, as they think proper, in the President alone, in the Courts of Law, or in the Heads of Departments.

The President shall have Power to fill up all Vacancies that may happen during the Recess of the Senate, by granting Commissions which shall expire at the End of their next Session.

Modern Text of Article II Section II the Constitution of the United States

The President is the overall Commander of all the military forces of the United States as well as the State Militias when the situation requires.

Reprieves, as well as pardons, can be granted by the President for any offence against the United States expect in cases of impeachment.

With advice and approval of the Senate, the President can make treaties with other countries, provided that two thirds of the Senate agrees. He shall also appoint Ambassadors, public ministers, Judges of the Supreme Court and other positions that appointments are not provided for, but are created by law. Congress must, by law, confirm all appointments of lower officers, courts of law or Department heads. In the event of a person not being confirmed, the President must supply a new candidate.

The President can fill any vacant position during a recess of the Senate by granting a commission that will expire at the end of the new session. These will be referred to as recess appointments.

Original Text of Article II Section III the Constitution of the United States

He shall from time to time give to the Congress Information of the State of the Union, and recommend to their Consideration such Measures as he shall judge necessary and expedient; he may, on extraordinary Occasions, convene both Houses, or either of them, and in Case of Disagreement between them, with Respect to the Time of Adjournment, he may adjourn them to such Time as he shall think proper; he shall receive Ambassadors and other public Ministers; he shall take Care that the Laws be faithfully executed, and shall Commission all the Officers of the United States.

Modern Text of Article II Section III the Constitution of the United States

Once a year, the President will address the full Congress and present the State of the Union, and relate a future vision and direction for the United States. He can address one or both Houses during extraordinary circumstances and will mediate between the House of Representatives and the Senate if they do not agree.

Original Text of Article II Section IV the Constitution of the United States

The President, Vice President and all civil Officers of the United States, shall be removed from Office on Impeachment for, and Conviction of, Treason, Bribery, or other high Crimes and Misdemeanors.

Modern Text of Article II Section IV the Constitution of the United States

The President, Vice President and all civilian officers of the United States will be removed from office for treason, bribery, or serious crimes or misdemeanors.

Discussion

This Article is the outline for what is known as the Executive Branch. It consists of a President and a Vice President. This is the branch that in the modern sense hangs out in the White House for a few years and changes every four or eight years.

The original method of electing a President and Vice President are also outlined in this article, these were later amended, and contrary to popular opinion, these offices are not elected directly by the people.

They are elected by electors (this is the electoral college we hear about each Presidential Election night). We are used to the electors doing exactly what the voters in their State decided by popular vote, but they are under no obligation to actually have to do so.

We also see that the various States get a number of electors equal to the number of Senators and Representatives. The candidate with the most electors on election night wins!

Once the electors are chosen, according to this Article, they were to meet in their State to decide who would be President and who would be Vice President. Originally the person who got the most elector votes would be President and the second highest would be Vice President. We think that might make for a real change in the tone and tenor of Presidential Elections.

Typically these elections turn into giant slime fests with one side throwing mud, garbage and occasionally lies about their opposition. Imagine that. If the politician in second place had to work with the winner might these elections go differently?

The method of election changed with the 12th Amendment, which will be discussed later in this book. Perhaps there is a reasonable argument to be made to go back to this original method with the winner being the person with the most votes and the Vice President being the person with the second most. It is an interesting thing to ponder.

Arguably, one of the most important jobs the President has is to act as Commander in Chief of the

Military. This says that he has command authority over our entire armed forces. The founders wanted a civilian as the head of the military to prevent a military state from developing. It can be argued that this was to prevent the United States from developing into an imperialistic, expansionist Nation using its Military to expand the borders at every opportunity. Whatever the original reason was, the control of the military in this Nation ultimately resides with a civilian.

There is one aspect of the Presidency that is also brought up in this Article that is paramount to limiting the power of the Presidency. That is the Advice and Consent clause. This means that the President can only act with the help and approval of the United States Congress on a variety of issues. Many Presidents in recent years, both Republican and Democrat, have attempted to use Executive Orders to do things that really should have Congressional approval. This is something that the Congress should exercise its authority to change, however, in recent times, many Congressmen have been more concerned with re-election than expanding Presidential Powers, but that is just the opinion of two Veterans. If you disagree with us, the great thing about this Nation is that whole free speech thing. Please feel free to let us know if you feel we are wrong. We are happy to have the debate but please provide a reason. From those reasons we can establish a dialog and happily try to meet in the middle (if need be), or convince each other of the positions we hold and get the other to convert to your side.

The Article also discusses the responsibilities of the Presidency. The Founders were very specific about certain tasks belonging in this branch of the government. They did not want this office to be too powerful and they were cautious to give the President the power to be able to do things when the Congress was not in session, but they did not want the President to be able to do too much without the assistance of the other Branches. They really were drawing up instructions for the President that rode a fine line. You want this office to be able to accomplish things by themselves if need be, in times of national emergency, but you don't want that to go too far. We think they did a pretty good job all things considered. Their methodology has served us pretty well so far.

The only other portion of this Article is the methods by which the President, Vice President, or other civil officers such as Cabinet Secretaries can be impeached. These are important because if a President (or these other offices) overstep their bounds there is a way to bring them back to their Constitutional limits. Congress just needs to have the intestinal fortitude to do so.

Chapter 4
Article III

Article III of the Constitution of the United States lays out the structure, as well as the powers of the Judicial Branch. This is the branch of government containing the Supreme Court as well as all lower courts. It is the watchdog (if we can use that term) for most everything that goes on in this Country to ensure Constitutionality/legality.

Original Text of Article III Section I the Constitution of the United States

The judicial Power of the United States shall be vested in one supreme Court, and in such inferior Courts as the Congress may from time to time ordain and establish. The Judges, both of the supreme and inferior Courts, shall hold their Offices during good Behaviour, and shall, at stated Times, receive for their Services a Compensation, which shall not be diminished during their Continuance in Office.

Modern Text of Article III Section I the Constitution of the United States

The Judicial Power of the United States shall reside in one Supreme Court as well as any inferior courts that the Congress may establish. The Judges at the Supreme Court and lower courts shall hold their offices during times of good behavior, for life, without the need of reappointment. The judges of all courts shall receive compensation for their service, which cannot be lowered at any point during their time in office.

Original Text of Article III Section II the Constitution of the United States

The judicial Power shall extend to all Cases, in Law and Equity, arising under this Constitution, the Laws of the United States, and Treaties made, or which shall be made, under their Authority;--to all Cases affecting Ambassadors, other public Ministers and Consuls;--to all Cases of admiralty and maritime Jurisdiction;--to Controversies to which the United States shall be a Party;--to Controversies between two or more States;-- between a State and Citizens of another State,--between Citizens of different States,--between Citizens of the same State claiming Lands under Grants of different States, and between a State, or the Citizens thereof, and foreign States, Citizens or Subjects.

In all Cases affecting Ambassadors, other public Ministers and Consuls, and those in which a State shall be Party, the supreme Court shall have original Jurisdiction. In all the other Cases before mentioned, the supreme Court shall have appellate Jurisdiction, both as to Law and Fact, with such Exceptions, and under such Regulations as the Congress shall make.

The Trial of all Crimes, except in Cases of Impeachment, shall be by Jury; and such Trial shall be held in the State where the said Crimes shall have been committed; but when not committed within any State, the Trial shall be at such Place or Places as the Congress may by Law have directed.

Modern Text of Article III Section II the Constitution of the United States

The power of the Judicial Branch shall apply to all cases both in Law and in Equity that apply under this Constitution, the Laws of the United States, and treaties that shall be made under their authority.

The power of the Judicial Branch shall apply to all cases affecting Ambassadors, or other public officials whose office is meant to look after the commercial interests of the citizenry while in other countries.

The power of the Judicial Branch shall apply to all cases of maritime jurisdiction.

The power of the Judicial Branch shall be to decide controversies to which the United States is a party. These include controversies between two or more States, between a State and citizens of another State, between citizens of different States, between citizens of the same State claiming lands under grants of different States, and between a State or the citizens of a State and foreign states citizens or subjects.

The Supreme Court has jurisdiction over all cases affecting Ambassadors, other public caretakers such as Consuls, and those in which one of the States is a Party to the action. The Supreme Court shall be the court of final appeal, there is no higher court and their decisions are the final decision on any matter brought before them for decision. The only recourse after their decision is to petition Congress to change the law.

The trial of all crimes, with the exception of Impeachment, shall be by Jury. The trial for any crime will be held in the State where it was committed. If a crime was not committed within any State the trial shall be at a place or places that the Congress has directed by Law.

Original Text of Article III Section III the Constitution of the United States

Treason against the United States, shall consist only in levying War against them, or in adhering to their Enemies, giving them Aid and Comfort. No Person shall be convicted of Treason unless on the Testimony of two Witnesses to the same overt Act, or on Confession in open Court.

The Congress shall have Power to declare the Punishment of Treason, but no Attainder of Treason shall work Corruption of Blood, or Forfeiture except during the Life of the Person attainted.

Modern Text of Article III Section III the Constitution of the United States

Treason against the United States will be defined as levying War against them by being devoted to an enemy, or by giving an enemy aid and comfort. No person will be convicted of Treason unless there is testimony of two witnesses to the same over Act or, upon their Confession in open Court.

The Congress has the power to declare the punishment for Treason. No one guilty of treason shall be punished except during the life of the person. Their ancestors cannot be held to account for their crime(s).

Discussion

This Article gives the framework to the Judicial Branch in just three small sections.

In the first section we learn all about the federal court system and that there can be only one (said in a Scottish accent directly out of a fantastic movie about some immortals) Supreme Court. They are the court of final authority. There is no higher court in the land and their word is final. There is no appealing to your mother, no calling grandma this time…this is the final word on the issue.

In this section we learn there must be a Chief Justice who presides over the court but the Founders did not say how many court members there would be.

The number of justices has grown over the years. Some would argue that it should grow again. We believe that there should be a higher bar set for Justices to be confirmed. Far too often now they are chosen on how they will decide on a single issue. We are not a single issue Nation. The Constitution is the their guide, therefore it should be what matters. Sadly, politics takes the place of common sense all too often.

Interestingly, the Founders did not say that there have to be any lower courts, or how many there should be. That power is left to the Congress to decide. In other words the Congress can create, as well as dissolve, the lower courts.

The Founders also did not want the Justices to be subject to political pressures of reelection. They, in fact, said that Justices serve for the remainder of their lives, unless they are convicted or impeached by Congress.

We also find out something that is not widely known, that the Supreme Court can hear any case for the first time, meaning a lower court need not hear the case at all. That was actually unknown to us.

There are some cases floating around that it is known will end up at the Supreme Court before a final decision is made. We find ourselves wondering why the spectacle, time, money (including tax dollars), and effort is wasted at the lower courts if the end is going to be a Supreme Court decision. Why not go straight to what is the ultimate destination on these issues.

There was a Presidential election a few years ago that we seemed to need this starting point. Why, in Florida, did they even bother going through all the other Courts. There was no way that election was going to end without a Supreme Court decision (or two) to sort out the mess. Agree or disagree with that election the Supreme Court is the final decision making authority on these things. The thing that routinely separates the United States from some other Nations is the peaceful transition of power. A Constitutional question arose during that transition, and an election ended with a new President and not with rifles, bullets, and mayhem.

The final section of this Article outlines treason. It explains what constitutes treason as well as the level of evidence that is needed in order to convict someone of that crime. The Founders knew the act of treason was important and not a trivial action taken. The Founders took treason very seriously and they expected future generations to do the same.

Chapter 5
Article IV

Article IV of the Constitution of the United States lays out the responsibilities and duties of the States of the Union as well as the Federal Government.

Original Text of Article IV Section I the Constitution of the United States

Full Faith and Credit shall be given in each State to the public Acts, Records, and judicial Proceedings of every other State. And the Congress may by general Laws prescribe the Manner in which such Acts, Records and Proceedings shall be proved, and the Effect thereof.

Modern Text of Article IV Section I the Constitution of the United States

Full confidence and trust will be given to each State in the area of public actions, record keeping and legal procedures by every other State. The Congress may decide how those beliefs and trusts will be proven and their results.

Original Text of Article IV Section II the Constitution of the United States

The Citizens of each State shall be entitled to all Privileges and Immunities of Citizens in the several States.

A Person charged in any State with Treason, Felony,

or other Crime, who shall flee from Justice, and be found in another State, shall on Demand of the executive Authority of the State from which he fled, be delivered up, to be removed to the State having Jurisdiction of the Crime.

No Person held to Service or Labour in one State, under the Laws thereof, escaping into another, shall, in Consequence of any Law or Regulation therein, be discharged from such Service or Labour, but shall be delivered up on Claim of the Party to whom such Service or Labour may be due.

Modern Text of Article IV Section II the Constitution of the United States

Everyone will have the same identical, and indistinguishable rights and privileges in each and every State of the Union.

A person, who has been found guilty of a felony, treason or other crime and escapes from justice of one State but is caught in another, will be sent back to the State from which the person escaped upon request of the Executive leadership of the original State.

A person held to service or labor in one State, under the Laws of the State, who escapes into another, shall not be discharged from such service or labor, but shall be delivered up upon a claim by the party to whom such service or labor is due.

Original Text of Article IV Section III the Constitution of the United States

New States may be admitted by the Congress into this Union; but no new State shall be formed or erected within the Jurisdiction of any other State; nor any State be formed by the Junction of two or more States, or Parts of States, without the Consent of the Legislatures of the States concerned as well as of the Congress.

The Congress shall have Power to dispose of and make all needful Rules and Regulations respecting the Territory or other Property belonging to the United States; and nothing in this Constitution shall be so construed as to Prejudice any Claims of the United States, or of any particular State.

Modern Text of Article IV Section III the Constitution of the United States

Congress can allow the admittance of new States into the United States. No State or States can be made within or from another State or merge two or more States or sections of States without the agreement of both State governances and the Congress.

Congress has the power to make rules and guidelines concerning territories and lands belonging to the government of the United States. This Constitution should not be used to change any claim of the United States or any specific State.

Original Text of Article IV Section IV the Constitution of the United States

The United States shall guarantee to every State in this Union a Republican Form of Government, and shall protect each of them against Invasion; and on Application of the Legislature, or of the Executive (when the Legislature cannot be convened), against domestic Violence.

Modern Text of Article IV Section IV the Constitution of the United States

The Federal Government will let the States elect their own government and will protect each State from hostile takeover by another State.

Discussion

Section one is referred to as the Full Faith and Credit Clause. This clause says that each State in the Union must extend validity to public acts, court proceedings, and records of other States. Congress is given the power to determine how this happens.

This way, in the more modern sense, if you are licensed to drive in one state you are licensed to drive in every other state. In reality this goes far beyond driver's licenses this is merely given as an example.

There are some notable exceptions to this like concealed carry weapons permits, but that is a debate for another day.

Section two discusses the responsibilities of the States under the Constitution. It outlines the privileges and immunities that States must give one another. The Founders thought it was important that States must be obligated to extradite criminals back to the States from which they fled.

This one is simple to imagine why it was done. If you rob a bank just inside the borders of New York, then walk across the border (perhaps a distance measured in feet depending on the bank) into another State, well, then New York has no right to ask you to come back. Not true says the

Constitution.

The Founders had large disagreements over one subject area, and the Country later fought a Civil War over the subject of slavery. In clause three of section two they wrote a fugitive slave clause. Some of the States in the original Union did not condone or permit slavery. This clause said that if a slave ran away to another State they would have to be sent back, no matter if the State the slave ran to had Slaves or not. This clause is no longer relevant today as slavery was abolished thanks to the 13th Amendment.

As this Article was all about States and their roles and responsibilities there was one thing the federal government offered them in return. The States were guaranteed a government that would be a republic.

In many ways the original intent was for as little governing as practical to be done at the federal level. The States, therefore, had certain responsibilities to one another and the Union and the Founding Fathers wanted to be sure that they put that in writing so there was no confusion.

Over the years, some argue, that the Federal Government has expanded its role and the States have diminished theirs. That, in some cases, is probably true but that is why we have this document so that if one organization or another (State or Federal) goes outside the Constitutional Guidelines we have a way to rectify the situation.

It is a pretty ingenious series of checks and balances.

Chapter 6

Article V

Article V of the Constitution of the United States lays out the mechanism for making changes, or amendments to the Constitution. The Founders knew that they would never be able to anticipate all of the needs of future generations. It is for that reason they knew it was necessary to put in a mechanism for updates, or changes, to the Constitution.

Original Text of Article V of the Constitution of the United States

The Congress, whenever two thirds of both Houses shall deem it necessary, shall propose Amendments to this Constitution, or, on the Application of the Legislatures of two thirds of the several States, shall call a Convention for proposing Amendments, which, in either Case, shall be valid to all Intents and Purposes, as Part of this Constitution, when ratified by the Legislatures of three fourths of the several States, or by Conventions in three fourths thereof, as the one or the other Mode of Ratification may be proposed by the Congress; Provided that no Amendment which may be made prior to the Year One thousand eight hundred and eight shall in any Manner affect the first and fourth Clauses in the Ninth Section of the first Article; and that no State, without its Consent, shall be deprived of its equal

Suffrage in the Senate.

Modern Text of Article V of the Constitution of the United States

Amendments to this Constitution can be made when either the Congress by two thirds majority of both houses deem it necessary or when the Legislatures of two thirds majority of the several States call for a Convention for proposing Amendments. In either case, these amendments will be considered as part of this Constitution when ratified by the Legislatures of three fourth of the States.

No amendment may be made prior to the year one thousand eight hundred and eight that shall affect the first and fourth clauses in the ninth section of the first article. No State, without its consent, shall be deprived of its equal voting rights in the Senate.

Discussion

The Founders were certain that they had no way to anticipate all of the needs of governance for future generations. For that reason they put a mechanism in the Constitution for updates, or to use a modern word, upgrades. To use an even more modern phrase, the Constitution is to be considered a "Living Document."

However, they were also certain that they wanted those updates to the Constitution to be well thought out, and to be, truly, the will of the citizenry. So if you read this passage and really think about it they wanted was to make sure that an amendment was a hard thing to get added to this founding document. It isn't easy to do, but is from time to time needed.

In fact, the Founders themselves decided right away their document wasn't perfect. The States would only ratify it if a package of amendments were added right away. We call these ten amendments the Bill of Rights and it will be discussed later in this book.

In recent history it is typically the Amendments that cause all the controversy and discussion. It is going to be very obvious in later sections of this book which ones cause us the most...disagreement. Could the second Amendment be one such source of National arguments? Read that chapter and find out!

Chapter 7
Article VI

Article VI of the Constitution of the United States says, among other things, that the newly formed United States of America will be responsible for all of the debts incurred by the government under the Articles of Confederation. This was "housekeeping" of a sort. They didn't feel it was proper to just ignore debts of the past. They also wanted to put some specificity on paper as to what authority was now in effect, and which laws were the dominant ones of the Nation. The Founders also chose to call out and ensure a lack of religious requirement for governmental leadership roles, something that was virtually unheard of in the days when this was written.

Original Text of Article VI of the Constitution of the United States

All Debts contracted and Engagements entered into, before the Adoption of this Constitution, shall be as valid against the United States under this Constitution, as under the Confederation.

This Constitution, and the Laws of the United States which shall be made in Pursuance thereof; and all Treaties made, or which shall be made, under the Authority of the United States, shall be the supreme Law of the Land; and the Judges in every State shall be bound thereby, any Thing in the Constitution or

Laws of any State to the Contrary notwithstanding.

The Senators and Representatives before mentioned, and the Members of the several State Legislatures, and all executive and judicial Officers, both of the United States and of the several States, shall be bound by Oath or Affirmation, to support this Constitution; but no religious Test shall ever be required as a Qualification to any Office or public Trust under the United States.

Modern Text of Article VI of the Constitution of the United States

All debts incurred or obligations entered into, before the adoption of this Constitution, shall be considered valid debts or agreements with the United States of America under the Constitution, just as they were under the Articles of Confederation.

This Constitution, and the laws of the United States made as a result of it, and all treaties made under the authority of the United States are the supreme Law of the land. The judges in every State shall be bound by these laws, in spite of the laws of any State to the contrary.

The Senators, Representatives, Members of the several State Legislatures, and all Executive as well as Judicial Officers of both the United States and the several States shall swear an Oath to support this Constitution. No religious test shall ever be required as a qualification to any office or public trust under the United States.

Discussion

This one is pretty easy. The Founders knew that the

Confederation had debts and those debts needed to be paid. Shay's rebellion was, largely, as a result of those debts not being paid. Historically, they had precedent that they didn't want to see repeated.

They also wanted to make sure that future generations understood that federal laws that were passed and deemed to be Constitutional are the supreme laws of the land. In other words, if there was a State law that were passed which stood contrary to a Federal Law, it is the Federal Law that is valid and the State Law is overruled. It was kind of like adult supervision to the States in way if you think about it.

Somewhere there is a History Professor with their head exploding as we write that paragraph but this is the way WE see it. It is possible to complicate what the Founders did and write 1,000 page dissertations on the topic, but it boils down to who is in charge and in this case it is the Federal Government who is the supreme law of the land, or the grownup in the room.

The final, closing part of this Article wants to be sure that people understand the supremacy of the Federal Laws. It ensures that Judges, Governors and other people in positions of authority understand that the Constitution is the final authority by swearing an oath that they will support this document during the course of doing their job.

The Founders were big on oaths. They felt that a person's word was important. This practice is something that carries over to this day when you swear an oath in court to tell the truth, the whole truth and absolutely nothing but the truth!

It is historically interesting that, at least in this Country, this precedent was in the law from the very first day.

Chapter 8
Article VII

Article VII of the Constitution of the United States is the ratification requirements and signatures. Think about the end of every legal document you have ever seen, or perhaps your annual income tax return. There is always a section that explains by signing the document it becomes valid. This section basically says, you guys sign this, the States agree and this is now the supreme law of the land.

Original Text of Article VII of the Constitution of the United States

The Ratification of the Conventions of nine States, shall be sufficient for the Establishment of this Constitution between the States so ratifying the Same.

The Word, "the," being interlined between the seventh and eighth Lines of the first Page, the Word "Thirty" being partly written on an Erazure in the fifteenth Line of the first Page, The Words "is tried" being interlined between the thirty second and thirty third Lines of the first Page and the Word "the" being interlined between the forty third and forty fourth Lines of the second Page.

Attest William Jackson Secretary

done in Convention by the Unanimous Consent of the States present the Seventeenth Day of September in the Year of our Lord one thousand seven hundred and Eighty seven and of the Independance of the United States of America the Twelfth In witness whereof We have hereunto subscribed our Names,

Modern Text of Article VII of the Constitution of the United States

This ratification of the convention of nine States shall be sufficient to establish this Constitution between the States.

This was done in convention by the unanimous consent of the States present on the seventeenth day of September in the year of our Lord one thousand seven hundred and eighty seven. We have voted on this Constitution and inscribed our names,

Discussion

This article was pretty simple, yet very necessary. It is the one that explains how many States must agree to this document for it to be validated. The Founders decided upon nine, or nine out of thirteen. It turned out the results were better than nine but they felt a larger than one half agreement was needed.

The Founders were very detail oriented people and they took every effort in crafting this document to be sure that a clear majority of people agreed upon general decisions and how the leadership of the new Nation would decide the laws that everyone must live under.

They did not want to have the country fall into a tyrannical form of government. The requirements put forth in the Constitution was their very best attempt at avoiding that possibility.

Chapter 9

Amendment I

This marks the start of The Bill of Rights, or the first Ten Amendments to the Constitution. These were things that weren't included in the original text but the Founders immediately decided needed to be added for ratification.

Original Text of the First Amendment to the Constitution of the United States

Congress shall make no law respecting an establishment of religion, or prohibiting the free exercise thereof; or abridging the freedom of speech, or of the press; or the right of the people peaceably to assemble, and to petition the Government for a redress of grievances.

Modern Text of the First Amendment to the Constitution of the United States

Congress will not pass any law that establishes a national religion or prohibiting someone from practicing any religion.

Congress will not pass any law preventing the freedoms of speech or of the press. Citizens should be free to say or publish anything they see fit. Other citizens are free to read or not read anything they see fit.

Congress will not pass any law preventing the

citizenry to peacefully assemble.

Congress will not pass any law preventing the citizenry from petitioning their Government for changes to a policy or law that may be unfairly treating the citizens of The United States of America.

Discussion

This Amendment is one of the commonly quoted ones if you access the Internet or watch the nightly news. Sometimes it isn't even quoted correctly but let's not worry about misquotes for the moment. Usually it is just referred to as that guarantee to freedom of speech.

There is a famous question that runs around about this Amendment and sadly we do not know the origin.

Does the freedom of speech extend to the ability to run into a crowded theater and scream "FIRE"!

No, of course not. That isn't free speech...that is just moronic behavior that is very likely to get someone hurt as the crowd rushes for the door. The Founders were not talking about that kind of thing. They were talking about the ability to say things that were in opposition to a policy, procedure, or in some other way speak out against the government (or some other entity). They weren't talking about just saying whatever you want. We do have slander laws in this country, and they are Constitutional.

Politically speaking, there are times when speech is even equated to money. There has been an argument for many years that speech in politics means that very large donors should be able to donate whatever amount they want to whomever they want. That is then called "free speech," because that money allows that political donation recipient to buy HUGE amounts of advertising thereby allowing loud free speech.

It is an interesting argument and logically it holds true. However, in interest of full disclosure, we feel that up to the minute (or near real time, say within days of the act) donation lists to candidates with names and amounts listed should be available via the Internet. That way the voting public will know who is enabling the speech and thereby permit a more accurate decision when figuring out who we want to vote for.

Let's play out an example. Imagine that Charles Manson (when he was alive) had a huge fortune. He used that fortune to help get a President elected. That President would then have the power of the pardon and owe Charles a big favor.

If money really is free speech we should be able to know who is speaking. There is no guarantee of anonymity.

At is basic level, what this Amendment means to us is that people are free to print, publish, or even say whatever they want.

Other people are free to sue them if they think that person has caused them harm (professionally for instance).

Another interesting thing that is often seen in the modern world is that there are calls to silence certain media personalities. Usually some talk show host that may have gone into the land of saying things that isn't something that a large number of people agree with. So the answer we tend towards these days is "Let's get that guy off the air."

Let us give the opinion of at least these two veterans. We think people are free to say whatever they want...on television, on the radio, wherever. As a citizen I am free to not listen. Running boycotts usually only increases the ratings of the person who was the offending party. Stop giving these shock jocks the free press and they might stop doing these things.

We recommend that if you think a celebrity, talk show host or other person with access to the media has said something that you find in opposition to what you agree with, don't go to the media complaining about that person. Change the channel. Then write Letters to the Editor, write for a website, start a blog, spread the word of what you believe in. In other words, exercise your freedom of speech and press (electronic press in the modern sense). That is how we solve problems Constitutionally.

What freedom of speech means, is that each person has the absolute right to state their belief at the top of their lungs, while another person has the right to shout at the top of their lungs how wrong the first person it, or merely state their own opinion (usually more effective). If you are offended by what is said, leave, turn the channel, put the book down, or visit a different web site. It is that simple.

What freedom of speech does NOT mean is that one person will hold their belief over another by way of legal system (which is commonly attempted these days). People commonly will use "Freedom of Speech" to force their own agenda's upon others. As an example there was a person who sued a school system due to the mandatory reciting of the "Pledge of Allegiance" because the pledge has the word God in it (the person doing the suing was atheist). As we have stated, if you are offended, leave, don't say that one word, ask to be excused from the activity, but don't make the whole situation a media spectacle. Have some respect for OTHER people's right to freedom of speech.

This also goes for the other aspects brought forth in this amendment, Freedom of Press. We both agree that there can be instances where the written word is very strong and can cause some uncomfortable feelings. Written dialog is used to convey feelings, situations, drama as well as news on which of the latest celebrities are showing their butts in New Jersey, or some other trivial matter involving a wardrobe malfunction.

We as a nation have the responsibility to express our views, beliefs and stories (of what ever type), pass on news (both good and bad) while having the common sense to be decent about it. Not everyone needs to hear on the 6pm news the f-bomb dropped 6 times because the local convenience store got robbed.

The clause about peaceful gathering is also mentioned. As Veterans, we know both peaceful and non-peaceful gatherings. In ALL sense of the phrases, we suggest peaceful ones. Trust us, it's a better idea.

We could cite many passages from Gandhi or Martin

Luther King Jr. but I think our point is made. If a peaceful group were to meet and voice their ideas in a calm way, the opposition would be more inclined to give them the proper respect and listen to their argument. Once bricks, rocks, chairs, cars etc start getting used as projectiles, it loses all credibility and becomes a riot.

Peaceful gathering good, riot bad.

Finally we find that we have the right for any and all citizens to petition the Government to propose or amend a law or ruling, which a person or group may find unfair. This is really a great Country. If you don't like a law you can suggest a modification, annulment or a new law.

Chapter 10

Amendment II

Original Text of the Second Amendment to the Constitution of the United States

A well-regulated Militia, being necessary to the security of a free State, the right of the people to keep and bear Arms, shall not be infringed.

Modern Text of the Second Amendment to the Constitution of the United States

A well maintained, and regulated civilian armed Paramilitary (Militia) is needed to provide security to the country. The people have a right to own and keep firearms and this right will not be taken away or lessened.

Discussion

This Amendment has probably been the subject of more news cycles and opinion shows than any other.

We feel it necessary to go into this discussion with a disclaimer. We want to reiterate that we are both veterans. We have both fired, and owned, many different firearms in our lifetime. We have both fired, but not owned, automatic weapons in our lifetime (we were both in the Army after all).

That being said there are a LOT of strange opinions on this subject of keeping and bearing arms. Interestingly that part of this amendment is always quoted but the remainder of it seems to be missing from that discussion. We believe the entire thing must be examined to understand the intent.

We have heard the extremes.

One of the interesting extremes is that the Founders meant that you should have access to muskets (after all, when this document was written muskets WERE considered the assault weapons of the day). Well, let's just say we disagree with that.

As an interesting side note, or question. We feel it necessary to ask. What weapon on this planet is not capable of assault? If you can't assault someone with an object, by definition, it isn't a weapon. So, let's just admit that a so-called "assault weapons ban" is really just a step towards attempting to take away all guns, although you should really throw hammers, knives, and many others into that same category as assault weapons.

The other extreme says that if the military has access to it, a citizen should have access to it.

Well, playing this argument out means that the starting shortstop for any major league baseball team should be able to buy an F-16 (their salaries are high enough), or perhaps some surface to air missiles.

Maybe grandma wants a heavy machine-gun mounted on her 1984 Road-Master station wagon?

What if that quiet guy at the end of the street wants an Anti-tank rocket to start taking pot shots at those annoying punk kids and their loud rock and or roll music?

—

We might see little Suzy-Q sitting in her window one day with a 50 caliber sniper rifle shooting at the neighbors cats when they cross the fence line?

Should these things be allowed?

We both have to say no.

Should we have limits on what those arms that the general public has access to be?

We think there should be, and in fact in current law there are limitations.

Should those limits be more extreme than they are?

Should those limits be less extreme than they are?

That is the subject that MUST be discussed through that freedom of speech aspect of the Constitution we covered under 1st Amendment. We will not render a personal opinion other than to say that the citizenry should be able to keep and bear arms, just as the Founders said. There should also be a clear definition in law of what that means.

The discussion-taking place has to be an informed discussion. John Doe who has read a military book or viewed weapons being fired on the Internet is NOT an expert on the subject. Someone saying they have seen two hundred weapons fired in their lifetime is not an expert nor is an organization, whose mission is to promote the ownership of weapons.

While these people or groups may say they are experts, many are not. An expert is someone who has used, and maintained, a weapon over a long period of time. Those are the people who need to have a voice in all matters relating to weapons and the

Second Amendment, as should every American but we need to be honest about expertise as part of that discussion. We must exercise our free speech and have our opinions heard but we must also understand who is spouting the other opinions we hear. Sometimes the source is of equal importance to the message.

We have a proposal on this subject. Let's all sit down and have a RATIONAL discussion on this subject. Not one where an invitation to talk about this subject is sent by one side and pictures a bear that the invitee shot to death are sent back as an RSVP (that actually happened).

Chapter 11

Amendment III

Original Text of the Third Amendment to the Constitution of the United States

No Soldier shall, in time of peace be quartered in any house, without the consent of the Owner, nor in time of war, but in a manner to be prescribed by law.

Modern Text of the Third Amendment to the Constitution of the United States

Soldiers cannot take over a privately owned home or stay in a privately owned home unless the owner agrees, without duress, either in peacetime or during armed conflict.

Soldiers must act within all accordances of the laws of personal ownership.

Discussion

This Amendment was, and is today, very probably the least controversial and least discussed in the Constitution.

It basically says you cannot force a homeowner of any nation to give soldiers a place to live.

This came about as a result of the British Army coming into areas (such as Boston) and taking over private residences to house their troops. The Founders wanted to make sure that this new government and army would never do such a thing.

Chapter 12

Amendment IV

Original Text of the Fourth Amendment to the Constitution of the United States

The right of the people to be secure in their persons, houses, papers, and effects, against unreasonable searches and seizures, shall not be violated, and no Warrants shall issue, but upon probable cause, supported by Oath or affirmation, and particularly describing the place to be searched, and the persons or things to be seized.

Modern Text of the Fourth Amendment to the Constitution of the United States

Law enforcement shall not, without having a specified reason, search or seize any personal items of a citizen. Probable cause has to be stated clearly and in detail describe what is being searched for and where these things are being searched for, and it must be taken to the legal authority before any search and seizure can be done and a warrant issued. Every reasonable effort must be taken to explain the purpose of the search and seizure prior to it taking place.

Discussion

This Amendment gets a large amount of press attention in this post 9/11 world. Actually, it should probably be discussed (and enforced) more.

Thanks to the Global War on Terror the United States has passed things such as The Patriot Act, with the best of intentions at the time.

Now we are faced with a situation where we have the NSA keeping track of phone records and doing "things" with the data.

So, that brings us to the controversial part. Some of our Congress people, and certainly two Presidents have thought that these types of things are ok for them to do. There are probably rooms full of government lawyers who have said, yeah...sure...no problem, we can do that. The Constitution has some loopholes in the syntax, so why not.

Why is that?

Well, this Amendment says that you can't search or seize any PERSONAL items belonging to a citizen. Most of what has been done is seizing of phone records, or recording of telephone conversations.

The argument on the government side is, and neither of the authors recall hearing the government side of this one the news so we are just assuming this, is that the cellular phone network, or telephone landline switching network is not your PERSONAL property. You rent use of it.

Then the government gets a special court order allowing it, which you need not have knowledge of because you don't own the line. The phone company knows about it, but they are under no obligation to tell you.

The Founders put this Amendment in, or so others, not us, have argued it so that someone's home and personal records inside that home can't be taken away and examined without a warrant.

So, does that mean that the government has the right to things transmitted across these phone networks, or perhaps e-mail networks?

They seem to think it does.

Do we agree with that?

Well personally we won't say if we agree with it or not. However, we will say that there are certain things that should never be in an email, things that should never be in a text message. There are ways to keep these things private. Perhaps, talking face to face with someone (imagine that). Sending them a physical (or snail mail) letter. These are things you can easily keep private, at least until the arguments about these laws we live with today can be heard out in the public square and judges can make decisions.

We will say that if you want to talk about it (back to that freedom of speech and press thing) we encourage you to do so, very regularly. Just remember, anything put onto the Internet, STAYS on the Internet. Nothing can be permanently deleted from the web. So be careful of those selfies you take.

We know, it isn't as fast to send snail mail, but remember we aren't here to sway your political leanings we are hear to present the Constitution and the reason certain things exist inside it.

Chapter 13

Amendment V

Original Text of the Fifth Amendment to the Constitution of the United States

No person shall be held to answer for a capital, or otherwise infamous crime, unless on a presentment or indictment of a Grand Jury, except in cases arising in the land or naval forces, or in the Militia, when in actual service in time of War or public danger; nor shall any person be subject for the same offence to be twice put in jeopardy of life or limb; nor shall be compelled in any criminal case to be a witness against himself, nor be deprived of life, liberty, or property, without due process of law; nor shall private property be taken for public use, without just compensation.

Modern Text of the Fifth Amendment to the Constitution of the United States

No one will be held for a crime unless so ordered by a grand jury or judge. The exception is the military forces during times of war or public danger. The military can also issue this order in those times mentioned.

A person shall *not* be tried for the same crime twice or be a witness against their own persons.

No one will have their life, liberty or property taken from them without legal judgment or have their personal belongs taken for public use without payment for those belongings.

Discussion

This Amendment is usually not one that is argued terribly often, with one notable exception.

It basically tells us that the police (or other government authority) can't hold a Citizen for an unreasonable amount of time (discussed below) without being charged of a crime. Being charged with a crime means there will be a trial. But, people will complain, there is a long time while the person is in confinement before their trial. This is due to the gathering of evidence phase, not because of anything else. You can argue what reasonable length of time is but that is where we must argue, not the validity or invalidity of being held.

In other words, despite what prime time television shows have told us, we can't be thrown in jail, have the key thrown out, and never see the light of day again. That is, without being charged with a crime.

As we mentioned this is usually not argued by too many people, as even drug dealers and murders see their day in court.

The notable exception to this is the prisoners from the Global War in Terror that to this day still reside at a prison at Guantanamo Bay Cuba. These prisoners went a very long time without being charged with anything. Here is the government argument for that exception.

They are not United States Citizens; they are not inside the United States and therefore not subject to our laws and privileges. They are, and this is where it gets sticky, on a Military Base. Those are generally considered US Territory. We really don't know exactly how that one is gotten around, but somehow it is.

On top of all of that they are considered to be Prisoners of War. While we are required by the Geneva Convention to treat them with basic human rights, they don't fall under our judicial system.

Is this government argument correct?

Maybe, but maybe not.

That is beyond the scope of this book and could probably fill book after book by itself (if you look on Amazon there may already be one). However, the Constitution does only apply to Citizens of the United States and really only to the area of the globe inside our borders.

The Constitution, and the rights guaranteed by it don't extend everywhere. For instance in Iran one cannot reasonably expect to have the right to indefinite detainment without being charged with a crime. There, you can be thrown into a prison for no apparent reason and the Constitution of the United States can't protect you, even if you are a US Citizen.

Another recent possible Fifth Amendment issue in the recent news cycles concerns the Internal Revenue Service. There was a controversy of them holding up and allegedly harassing groups with one (and only one) political ideology. That is the claim.

How true is that claim?

Well...enter the United States Congress doing an investigation (what could *possibly* go wrong now). The Congress questioned an IRS official, and that official "took the fifth" and refused to answer questions (presumably so they wouldn't incriminate themselves).

Here is the interesting bit.

That same official was offered immunity for any wrongdoing then pulled back in front of Congress. So, this amendment says you can refuse to answer so you don't incriminate yourself. This person can't possibly incriminate themselves in the commission of a crime...they have immunity.

So do Fifth Amendment rights pertain to this? Can this person officially refuse to answer questions without being held in contempt of Congress (for which they can be thrown in jail)?

It is an interesting Constitutional question.

Chapter 14

Amendment VI

Original Text of the Sixth Amendment to the Constitution of the United States

In all criminal prosecutions, the accused shall enjoy the right to a speedy and public trial, by an impartial jury of the State and district wherein the crime shall have been committed, which district shall have been previously ascertained by law, and to be informed of the nature and cause of the accusation; to be confronted with the witnesses against him; to have compulsory process for obtaining witnesses in his favor, and to have the Assistance of Counsel for his defence.

Modern Text of the Sixth Amendment to the Constitution of the United States

In all criminal matters, a person has the right to a fair and impartial trial within the State and District of the alleged crime.

Each person shall be informed of the nature of the crime for which they are accused and have witness presented both for, and against the person in question, and the accused will have the right to legal counsel for their defense.

Discussion

This Amendment is really a partner of the Fifth, in

our opinion. The Fifth says you have to be charged if you are to be detained.

This Amendment says after you are charged you need to have a trial and that trial must be fair.

You also have the right to a lawyer on your side, no matter what your income level is. These are the court appointed attorneys we hear so much about.

There are some cases we see links to on various social media websites that usually come along with the statement (paraphrasing), "skip the trial get a rope." Ok…sure, free speech, we get it. But the accused, no matter how good the evidence against them, deserves their day in court. Let the system work the way it is supposed to, that includes in cases when the guilt appears to be incontrovertible.

You, as a citizen, also get the right to face those testifying against you.

That last one is something the mafia really liked over the years. They used to find out who was testifying against them and intimidate this person in various ways. This eventually led to witness protection programs, but again, that is a story for a different book.

Whatever you think of this Amendment we are both very glad we live in a country where you still have these rights. There may, or may not, have been infringement of those rights on the Guantanamo prisoners but, as we discussed in the previous chapter, the argument is that these rights don't apply.

We can all get on board with the right to a lawyer.

However, we may not want someone to know we are testifying (for or against) in a particular trial. We can think of a few cases where if we had been a witnesses we would want to be anonymous but that isn't the way it works.

Our Country is one of the good ones, in that we guarantee these rights. We also know that there are countries in the world that do not guarantee you a speedy trial, much less all of these other things.

Let's hope we retain these rights into the future.

Chapter 15

Amendment VII

Original Text of the Seventh Amendment to the Constitution of the United States

In Suits at common law, where the value in controversy shall exceed twenty dollars, the right of trial by jury shall be preserved, and no fact tried by a jury, shall be otherwise re-examined in any Court of the United States, than according to the rules of the common law.

Modern Text of the Seventh Amendment to the Constitution of the United States

In lawsuits with a value of more than twenty dollars, a person has a right to a trial by jury. No case tried by a jury shall be tried a second time.

Discussion

This Amendment was added so that the Founders could guarantee a trial by jury for anyone accused of a crime.

Sometimes this is referred to as the double jeopardy amendment.

They also did not want people to have the fear of going back to court for the same exact crime a second time. Meaning, if you are tried for robbery and found not guilty, you can be tried if you commit a second robbery. You cannot be retired for the first robbery.

This particular Amendment is rarely controversial and we expect will remain part of the United States culture for as long as we have a Country.

There is a notable exception to this. You can't go to trial in a criminal court a second time. You can be sued in civil court. Think about OJ Simpson. He was found not guilty in criminal court but a civil court found that he was liable. In civil court the punishment was dollars not time in jail.

It does amaze us that most people tend towards civil trials these days, with the awards in the millions of dollars (if not MUCH higher). This is the court system (and trial lawyers) that is always in the news as needing reform. Some of the awards being as high as they are it causes people sue for lots of different reasons.

We won't render an opinion other than to say if reforms are going to happen in these cases we must introduce laws that will change these courts. So rather than just talking about it we urge all the talk show hosts who say, "we need reform" to call their representatives (State and Federal) and work with them on some legislation to change the situation. Isn't doing something about the problem better than just complaining about it? It is, after all, their Constitutional right to suggest a change if they are really as passionate about this as they claim.

Chapter 16

Amendment VIII

Original Text of the Eighth Amendment to the Constitution of the United States

Excessive bail shall not be required, nor excessive fines imposed, nor cruel and unusual punishments inflicted.

Modern Text of the Eighth Amendment to the Constitution of the United States

Incredibly high bails, fines or cruel and unusual punishments will not be used against a citizen.

Discussion

This very short amendment is the so-called cruel and unusual punishment aspect of life in these United States.

It says that if you are arrested for, and subsequently, convicted of a crime, that you can't be fined, or punished outrageously. We would argue that in some cases we might be coming close as a Nation to violating this, the last time I got a speeding ticket it was pretty bad. Ok, that was a joke, and one my wife is not going to find funny when she reads this.

Despite the bemoaning my inability to not read a highway speed limit sign, it is important that we can expect as citizens that the government can't dish out punishments that are totally unfitting of the crime.

They must be reasonable and just. We can argue reasonable and just but those conditions must be met, or the judgment against the guilty party could be considered Unconstitutional.

Chapter 17

Amendment IX

Original Text of the Ninth Amendment to the Constitution of the United States

The enumeration in the Constitution, of certain rights, shall not be construed to deny or disparage others retained by the people.

Modern Text of the Ninth Amendment to the Constitution of the United States

The enumeration in the Constitution of very specific rights shall not be used to deny or denigrate other rights retained by the people.

Discussion

This amendment is interesting for many reasons. There are legal scholars who will say that this is a very specific thing. We disagree.

This amendment was probably intended to limit government power. There is no evidence about what rights they were talking about when they said "other rights."

It doesn't give out a right, or take one away. It just makes a statement about rights in general.

Was it intended to limit government power?

Probably.

In the modern sense it is usually used to stop

government expansion of power. It was put in place, we think, as a way to catch future governments from expanding in ways they couldn't anticipate and further protect the citizenry from tyrannical leadership.

The Founders had a real interest in stopping the creeping growth of government power.

Perhaps *this* Amendment is a good topic for some radio talk show host to discuss at length as they tend to do with that second Amendment. Both are important but one seems to be forgotten.

Chapter 18

Amendment X

Original Text of the Tenth Amendment to the Constitution of the United States

The powers not delegated to the United States by the Constitution, nor prohibited by it to the States, are reserved to the States respectively, or to the people.

Modern Text of the Tenth Amendment to the Constitution of the United States

The powers not given to the Federal Government by the Constitution, or not prohibited by it, are powers for the States or the people themselves.

Discussion

This amendment is the State's rights portion of the Constitution. This basically says that whatever power does not reside in the federal government as a result of the Constitution resides in the States or with the People.

The original intent of this amendment was supposed to be to limit Congressional powers.

In the modern sense that hasn't been what it was used for. It has usually only added uncertainty about various rights.

This is one of the areas the Founders were vague, and perhaps that was done intentionally to allow future generations some flexibility in solving the problems they would be faced with in the best possible way for that period of time.

This is, between us, an Amendment that we feel could use some updating. Crafty lawyers have gotten ahold of it and likely permuted the original intent into something new. Perhaps this should be revisited and refined a bit. The States do have rights and we should allow them to be exercised more freely.

Chapter 19

Amendment XI

From this amendment forward we are no longer in The Bill of Rights. The remaining amendments were all added after the Founders had ratified the Constitution and we were living under its protections as a Nation.

Note: Passed by Congress March 4, 1794. Ratified February 7, 1795.

Original Text of the Eleventh Amendment to the Constitution of the United States

The Judicial power of the United States shall not be construed to extend to any suit in law or equity, commenced or prosecuted against one of the United States by Citizens of another State, or by Citizens or Subjects of any Foreign State.

Modern Text of the Eleventh Amendment to the Constitution of the United States

Legal power of the Federal Government won't be changed or extended to any other legal matter already ongoing against a person of any State by another State or citizen of a different country.

Discussion

We know, even in our modern version, is a bizarre sentence. In modernizing the original there is no good way to write this without writing paragraphs of text. We saved that for the discussion.

The history of this amendment is interesting. It was passed as a direct result of a court decision (Chisholm v Georgia, 2 U.S. 419, 1793).

Basically, there is only one interpretation of this Amendment we can come up with. If you Google this particular amendment you will find what we did on trips to the library. Scholars disagree on what it means (I know you are totally shocked by that, ok just kidding we weren't shocked either).

The explanation we think was intended here is that nobody can sue a State in federal court unless that State agrees that the person can.

Some people have said, and we agree, that if we aren't careful with this amendment it can lead to abuses.

Perhaps this one should be discussed under that freedom of speech and press thing we all learned about earlier in this book. We have some sneaky lawyers in this country always looking for an angle to exploit. We should be careful on occasion and ensure some of those angles (should they exist) are closed.

Chapter 20

Amendment XII

This amendment to the Constitution alters the method we do Presidential Elections. It should be read along with portions of the Article of the main body of the Constitution dealing with the executive branch, with the understanding that some portions of the original text have now been modified.

Note: Passed by Congress December 9, 1803. Ratified June 15, 1804.

A portion of Article II, section 1 of the Constitution was superseded by the 12th amendment.

Original Text of the Twelfth Amendment to the Constitution of the United States

The Electors shall meet in their respective states and vote by ballot for President and Vice-President, one of whom, at least, shall not be an inhabitant of the same state with themselves; they shall name in their ballots the person voted for as President, and in distinct ballots the person voted for as Vice-President, and they shall make distinct lists of all persons voted for as President, and of all persons voted for as Vice-President, and of the number of votes for each, which lists they shall sign and certify, and transmit sealed to the seat of the government of the United States, directed to the President of the Senate; -- the President of the Senate shall, in the presence of the Senate and House of Representatives, open all the certificates and the votes shall then be counted; -- The person having the greatest number of votes for President, shall be the President, if such number be a majority of the whole number of Electors appointed; and if no person have such majority, then from the persons having the highest numbers not exceeding three on the list of those voted for as President, the House of Representatives shall choose immediately, by ballot, the President. But in choosing the President, the votes shall be taken by states, the representation from each state having one vote; a quorum for this purpose shall consist of a member or members from two-thirds of the states, and a majority of all the states shall be necessary to a choice. [And if the House of Representatives shall not choose a President whenever the right of choice shall devolve upon them, before the fourth day of March next following, then the Vice-President shall act as President, as in case of the death or other constitutional disability of the President. --]* The person having the greatest number of votes as Vice-President, shall be the Vice-President, if such number be a majority of the whole number of Electors appointed, and if no person have a majority, then from the two highest numbers on the list, the Senate shall choose the Vice-President; a quorum for the purpose shall consist of two-thirds of the whole number of Senators, and a majority of the whole number shall be necessary to a choice. But no person constitutionally ineligible to the office of President shall be eligible to that of Vice-President of the United States.

Modern Text of the Twelfth Amendment to the Constitution of the United States

Each elector will vote within their own State for two people, one of which is not of their own State to become the President of the United States. They shall do this in writing.

Those ballots are then sent to the President of Congress to be tallied and recorded. The person with the most tallies becomes the President of the United States. The person with the second largest amount of tallies becomes the Vice President of the United States.

If there is no majority vote for the President, the House of Representatives will immediately choose the President. But those votes will be done by State (each state getting 1 vote).

If there is no majority for the office of Vice President, the Senate will take the top two names and select a Vice president by a two-thirds vote.

If there is no selection for the President by the Fourth of March, then the vice president will hold the office of President until one is elected.

If a person is ineligible to be the President of the United States, then that person cannot be the Vice President of the United States.

Discussion

This Amendment alters the way we do Presidential elections. It gives us something close to the modern elections where we have electors who are chosen by people.

It also goes through what happens in the event of an election that is in question (think Bush v Gore). It is clear in what it says, and I think, has been interpreted by the Supreme Court along with the original intent.

Interestingly, if one recalls all of the Florida recounts some interesting bits came out of those nights.

One of the candidates actually went on television and challenged the other to a "re-election" in the State of Florida. Where in the Constitution is this allowed? Shouldn't someone running for President understand that couldn't possibly have been constitutional?

In that election the other side did some equally neurotic (and likely Un-Constitutional) things. The Supreme Court eventually stepped in and did enforce Constitutional steps to ensure the outcome they saw as the correct path forward.

It appears as though the system worked. There are books written about that election and we won't go into it any deeper except to say it was certainly a Constitutional test. That test was passed. We had a peaceful transition from one President to another.

Now, if you agree with who won that election or not is another question.

What might be in question is the original intent, and we don't want to denigrate into a discussion about hanging chads but this gave us the elections we know and vote in every four years to decide who will be in the Oval Office. So far in our history we have peacefully transitioned power from one President to another. That is not something every country on the planet can claim.

Chapter 21
Amendment XIII

Note: Passed by Congress January 31, 1865. Ratified December 6, 1865.

A portion of Article IV, section 2, of the Constitution was superseded by the 13th amendment.

Original Text of Section I of the Thirteenth Amendment to the Constitution of the United States

Neither slavery nor involuntary servitude, except as a punishment for crime whereof the party shall have been duly convicted, shall exist within the United States, or any place subject to their jurisdiction.

Modern Text of Section I of the Thirteenth Amendment to the Constitution of the United States

Slavery or involuntary servitude will be illegal in the United States except in matters of punishment for a committed crime inside the United States or its territories.

Original Text of Section II of the Thirteenth Amendment to the Constitution of the United States

Congress shall have power to enforce this article by appropriate legislation.

Modern Text of Section II of the Thirteenth Amendment to the Constitution of the United States

Congress will enforce this law with appropriate

legislation.

Discussion

This amendment abolished slavery in the United States.

We hope that there is not a single person left who will say that slavery was a good thing.

We are glad this amendment exists and hope that no future generation over-turns it and brings back the abomination existed prior to the Civil War.

Slavery was deplorable and should have never been a reality. Hopefully it will never be a reality again.

Chapter 22
Amendment XIV

NOTE: Passed by Congress June 13, 1866. Ratified July 9, 1868.

Article I, section II, of the Constitution was modified by section II of the 14th amendment.

Portions of the Amendment were later modified by the 26th.

Original Text of Section I of the Fourteenth Amendment to the Constitution of the United States

All persons born or naturalized in the United States, and subject to the jurisdiction thereof, are citizens of the United States and of the State wherein they reside. No State shall make or enforce any law which shall abridge the privileges or immunities of citizens of the United States; nor shall any State deprive any person of life, liberty, or property, without due process of law; nor deny to any person within its jurisdiction the equal protection of the laws.

Modern Text of Section I of the Fourteenth Amendment to the Constitution of the United States

All citizens of the United States either born or naturalized are subject to the laws of the United States and the States in which they live. States may not make laws which remove from the citizens their rights and privileges of being a Citizen. No States will confine a person without legal due process nor deny anyone the right to due process under the law.

Original Text of Section II of the Fourteenth Amendment to the Constitution of the United States

Representatives shall be apportioned among the several States according to their respective numbers, counting the whole number of persons in each State, excluding Indians not taxed. But when the right to vote at any election for the choice of electors for President and Vice-President of the United States, Representatives in Congress, the Executive and Judicial officers of a State, or the members of the Legislature thereof, is denied to any of the male inhabitants of such State, being twenty-one years of age,* and citizens of the United States, or in any way abridged, except for participation in rebellion, or other crime, the basis of representation therein shall be reduced in the proportion which the number of such male citizens shall bear to the whole number of male citizens twenty-one years of age in such State.

Modern Text of Section II of the Fourteenth Amendment to the Constitution of the United States

The number of representatives in each state is selected by the number of voting males over the age of 21 years and citizens, but not involved in armed rebellion against the government of the United States or guilty of other crimes against federal laws. The number of males will be reduced by the number of representatives in proportion over the age of 21 years that have lost the right to vote.

Original Text of Section III of the Fourteenth Amendment to the Constitution of the United States

---

No person shall be a Senator or Representative in Congress, or elector of President and Vice-President, or hold any office, civil or military, under the United States, or under any State, who, having previously taken an oath, as a member of Congress, or as an officer of the United States, or as a member of any State legislature, or as an executive or judicial officer of any State, to support the Constitution of the United States, shall have engaged in insurrection or rebellion against the same, or given aid or comfort to the enemies thereof. But Congress may by a vote of two-thirds of each House, remove such disability.

Modern Text of Section III of the Fourteenth Amendment to the Constitution of the United States

No person shall hold elected office in either State or Federal government who has taken up arms or insurrection against the federal government of the United States. Congress with a two-thirds vote from each house can remove this restriction from a person.

Original Text of Section IV of the Fourteenth Amendment to the Constitution of the United States

The validity of the public debt of the United States, authorized by law, including debts incurred for payment of pensions and bounties for services in suppressing insurrection or rebellion, shall not be questioned. But neither the United States nor any State shall assume or pay any debt or obligation incurred in aid of insurrection or rebellion against the United States, or any claim for the loss or emancipation of any slave; but all such debts, obligations and claims shall be held illegal and void.

Modern Text of Section IV of the Fourteenth

Amendment to the Constitution of the United States

The United States government will not question the responsibility of public debt obtained as payment of military pensions or bounties in service in suppression of armed revolt.

The United States will not take on the debt of those who were in armed revolt against the United States. All claims of loss of income, debt, or loss of property and all obligations will be held as illegal and not the responsibility of the government of the United States.

Original Text of Section V of the Fourteenth Amendment to the Constitution of the United States

The Congress shall have the power to enforce, by appropriate legislation, the provisions of this article.

Modern Text of Section V of the Fourteenth Amendment to the Constitution of the United States

Congress and the federal government will enforce this amendment to the Constitution.

Discussion

This Amendment is the civil rights amendment; looking at the dates it we can notice that it was around the time of the Civil War. It was meant to protect the civil rights of all Americans regardless of their race or gender.

This was meant to overcome slavery and ensure that African Americans could be citizens. Prior to this there was some concern and even attempts at ensuring that former slaves could not gain citizenship.

This amendment was, of course, not the end of civil

rights inequalities. That would come much later (e.g. the 1960s) as a matter of law, and even later in the hearts and minds of some.

In the modern world we have really come past much of this sort of issue and skin color, race, gender or anything else you care to list really is held against someone. The modern world has built in safeguards to ensure that achievement is what matters.

These inequalities, undoubtedly, still exist in the minds of some people. There isn't much that can be done about that. However, in a legal sense, things are MUCH different than they once were, in in part as a result of this Amendment.

Chapter 23

Amendment XV

Note: Passed by Congress February 26, 1869. Ratified February 3, 1870.

Original Text of Section I of the Fifteenth Amendment to the Constitution of the United States

The right of citizens of the United States to vote shall not be denied or abridged by the United States or by any State on account of race, color, or previous condition of servitude—

Modern Text of Section I of the Fifteenth Amendment to the Constitution of the United States

The right to vote will not be denied due to race, color, or having previously been a slave.

Original Text of Section II of the Fifteenth Amendment to the Constitution of the United States

The Congress shall have the power to enforce this article by appropriate legislation.

Modern Text of Section 2 of the Fifteenth Amendment to the Constitution of the United States

Congress and the Federal government will enforce this amendment to the Constitution.

Discussion

This amendment was put in place as a result of the

Civil War.

There were all of these new citizens that were once slaves. In many cases the areas where they were once slaves the localities did not want to count them as citizens at all, much less allow them the right to vote.

This amendment was put in place to ensure ex-slaves the right to help decide the leadership of this nation was not in question. Period. They were citizens, they could vote.

There were all manner of tricks to try to keep them from the voting booth and something had to be done.

It was either this or much of what the Civil War was fought over (and an estimated 750,000-850,000 men died for) could have been lost.

For years there were a variety of tricks, traps and other hurdles for these people to vote. All of which are things that we wish had not happened. At least this amendment made them Unconstitutional.

It may have taken time to remove those hurdles but they were eventually removed and now everyone can vote without regard to skin color.

There is currently an argument being made about Voter ID, etc, however all of those are not discussions that are Constitutional in nature, and they don't have anything to do with race, or gender, or any other method of separating individuals, therefore will not be discussed here, but they should be rationally discussed by both major parties.

Chapter 24
Amendment XVI

NOTE: Passed by Congress July 2, 1909. Ratified February 3, 1913.

Article I, section 9, of the Constitution was modified by amendment 16.

Original Text of the Sixteenth Amendment to the Constitution of the United States

The Congress shall have power to lay and collect taxes on incomes, from whatever source derived, without apportionment among the several States, and without regard to any census or enumeration.

Modern Text of the Sixteenth Amendment to the Constitution of the United States

Congress can levy taxes on income regardless of type of income, without regard to the size of each State.

Discussion

With this addition comes the ability of Congress to decide how much of the American citizenry's income is due to the government in the form of taxes. Prior to this point they could tax other things (imports, etc) but the question of taxing income was problematic at best.

From this point forward Congress has a tax code that grows increasingly complex every single year. Taxes never seem to go down. Every few years we hear about record tax receipts coming into Washington DC.

There are different rates for different income levels, sure, and occasionally they are adjusted up or down for each category, but if you think about those up or down changes they are small by comparison to the amount of money that flows into Washington DC from American's with jobs. In other words the politicians play in the margins so that they can go on television and say, "Look we lowered taxes!" When in reality they moved it some minor amount.

We know that to keep a country like this one running revenue must be obtained, and neither of us think that is a bad thing. However, we need to be watchful as to where that money goes.

Recently in the news we read a story about a group of Solar Cells had been put in, at Government expense, into Manchester airport in New Hampshire. Turns out nobody checked to see if the placement of them would interfere with pilot visibility and the glare off the panels was blinding pilots for a large part of the afternoon (when solar cells are most effective).

So the government solution was covering them. Solar cells covered up so that the Sun won't glare off of them (or generate electricity) don't really serve a purpose.

Renewable energy is an important thing, but we must be cognizant of what happens to our tax dollars. We must ask, often, what kind of return on investment we are getting for these expenditures.

Perhaps, an income tax is important so the government can do things, but as Constitutionally abiding citizens we should pay very careful attention to how our taxes are spent.

That brings us back to that free speech thing again. If we are mad about it, let your Representative know. Speak out. Yell if you must, but make your voice heard.

By the way that flub with solar cells cost you and me $3.5 Million dollars, or roughly 1 penny per American. It isn't much but we all need to pinch our pennies these days before they are gone.

The question is how many of these 1-penny savings projects are there.

After working on this section we did have a fantasy of starting a national movement to repeal this amendment. Perhaps if we ever get to retire and have enough spare time we can work on that.

Chapter 25
Amendment XVII

NOTE: Passed by Congress May 13, 1912. Ratified April 8, 1913.

Article I, section 3, of the Constitution was modified by the 17th amendment.

Original Text of the Seventeenth Amendment to the Constitution of the United States

The Senate of the United States shall be composed of two Senators from each State, elected by the people thereof, for six years; and each Senator shall have one vote. The electors in each State shall have the qualifications requisite for electors of the most numerous branch of the State legislatures.

When vacancies happen in the representation of any State in the Senate, the executive authority of such State shall issue writs of election to fill such vacancies: Provided, That the legislature of any State may empower the executive thereof to make temporary appointments until the people fill the vacancies by election as the legislature may direct.

This amendment shall not be so construed as to affect the election or term of any Senator chosen before it becomes valid as part of the Constitution.

Modern Text of the Seventeenth Amendment to the Constitution of the United States

The Senate of the United States has two members from each state. The citizens of that State elect these Senators from their own State. Each term will be only six years and each Senator will get one vote. The State government will set the requirements for election of Senator.

If a Senate seat becomes open, the State executive (the Governor) can create an election to fill the opening provided the State Legislature has not granted the Governor the ability to make a temporary selection until a vote can take place to elect a new Senator.

This amendment will not affect any ongoing elections or terms of current Senator chosen before accepted as part of the Constitution.

Discussion

This amendment changed how we elect Senators. Prior to this point State Legislatures chose them.

In other words the process was as follow. The people elect the State Legislature they want, and it was the State Legislature that picked the Senators they want.

In theory this was a great way to do it, because if the State Legislature accurately represents the people in their district they will go along with their general wishes and pick the best candidate according to the will of the people. This was a great thing prior to newspapers, radio, and in the modern world the Internet.

Back before modern transportation, when a State was too large to go out and meet lots of voters this was great. How could someone cover all of Texas and meet people whose vote he was seeking on horseback in a reasonable amount of time? The answer is they couldn't. So, the Founders made the election of Senators up to the State office holders.

In the modern sense these elections were returned to the people...where they belong.

This is, after all, a government of the people, by the people, for the people.

Chapter 26

Amendment XVIII

Passed by Congress December 18, 1917. Ratified January 16, 1919. Repealed by amendment 21.

Original Text of Section I of the Eighteenth Amendment to the Constitution of the United States

After one year from the ratification of this article the manufacture, sale, or transportation of intoxicating liquors within, the importation thereof into, or the exportation thereof from the United States and all territory subject to the jurisdiction thereof for beverage purposes is hereby prohibited.

Modern Text of Section I of the Eighteenth Amendment to the Constitution of the United States

One year from the date of accepting this Amendment as part of the Constitution, the making, distilling, transporting, selling or consuming alcoholic beverages, bringing in, importing alcohol or exporting alcohol to or from the United States or its territories is illegal.

Original Text of Section II of the Eighteenth Amendment to the Constitution of the United States

The Congress and the several States shall have concurrent power to enforce this article by appropriate legislation.

Modern Text of Section II of the Eighteenth

Amendment to the Constitution of the United States

Congress and State Government will both have the power to enforce this law.

Original Text of Section III of the Eighteenth Amendment to the Constitution of the United States

This article shall be inoperative unless it shall have been ratified as an amendment to the Constitution by the legislatures of the several States, as provided in the Constitution, within seven years from the date of the submission hereof to the States by the Congress.

Modern Text of Section III of the Eighteenth Amendment to the Constitution of the United States

This amendment will not go into affect unless Congress has accepted it as part of the Constitution within seven years from the date of submission.

Discussion

We voted amongst the two of us and it was unanimous. This was the dumbest Amendment imaginable. Submit this sort of thing to a fiction novel publisher and you would be laughed at as it doesn't come close enough to being believable for people to buy that book. There were other ways to phrase this that came to mind, we are both ex-enlisted Soldiers, but we are trying to keep these discussion sections relatively free of curse words. In this case it was a challenge.

Chapter 27

Amendment XIX

<u>Passed by Congress June 4, 1919. Ratified August 18, 1920.</u>

Original Text of the Nineteenth Amendment to the Constitution of the United States

The right of citizens of the United States to vote shall not be denied or abridged by the United States or by any State on account of sex.

Congress shall have power to enforce this article by appropriate legislation.

Modern Text of the Nineteenth Amendment to the Constitution of the United States

The right to vote as a citizen of the United States will not be denied or changed by the United States or any state on account of what gender the citizen.

Congress shall enforce this law.

Discussion

Until 1910s or so many States still did not allow women the right to vote. This ranks up there on the stupidity level of the amendment outlawing alcoholic beverages.

Women should have been allowed to vote since the start of this Nation and we are glad this was added and the ludicrous practice of taking fifty percent of the voting public and shoving them aside ended.

Chapter 28

Amendment XX

Note: Passed by Congress March 2, 1932. Ratified January 23, 1933.

Article I, section IV, of the Constitution was modified by section II of this amendment. In addition, a portion of the twelfth amendment was superseded by section III.

Original Text of Section I of the Twentieth Amendment to the Constitution of the United States

The terms of the President and the Vice President shall end at noon on the 20th day of January, and the terms of Senators and Representatives at noon on the 3rd day of January, of the years in which such terms would have ended if this article had not been ratified; and the terms of their successors shall then begin.

Modern Text of Section I of the Twentieth Amendment to the Constitution of the United States

The newly elected President and Vice President shall take office on January 20th and the members of Congress will begin their terms on January 3rd on the year their terms are to begin.

Original Text of Section II of the Twentieth Amendment to the Constitution of the United States

The Congress shall assemble at least once in every

year, and such meeting shall begin at noon on the 3d day of January, unless they shall by law appoint a different day.

Modern Text of Section II of the Twentieth Amendment to the Constitution of the United States

Congress will meet at 12 Noon on January 3rd of each year unless the date is changed by law.

Original Text of Section III of the Twentieth Amendment to the Constitution of the United States

If, at the time fixed for the beginning of the term of the President, the President elect shall have died, the Vice President elect shall become President. If a President shall not have been chosen before the time fixed for the beginning of his term, or if the President elect shall have failed to qualify, then the Vice President elect shall act as President until a President shall have qualified; and the Congress may by law provide for the case wherein neither a President elect nor a Vice President shall have qualified, declaring who shall then act as President, or the manner in which one who is to act shall be selected, and such person shall act accordingly until a President or Vice President shall have qualified.

Modern Text of Section III of the Twentieth Amendment to the Constitution of the United States

The Vice President-elect shall act as President if the President-elect dies before he or she can take office, is found to be unqualified, or unable to hold the office of President. By law Congress can declare a situation where both the President and Vice President elect are unfit, unqualified or unable to hold their offices.

Congress will then select a person to act as President until a new President can be qualified.

Original Text of Section IV of the Twentieth Amendment to the Constitution of the United States

The Congress may by law provide for the case of the death of any of the persons from whom the House of Representatives may choose a President whenever the right of choice shall have devolved upon them, and for the case of the death of any of the persons from whom the Senate may choose a Vice President whenever the right of choice shall have devolved upon them.

Modern Text of Section IV of the Twentieth Amendment to the Constitution of the United States

If there is a case of a death of the President and Vice President at the same period of time, the Congress has the right to select a President by the House of Representatives and a Vice President by the Senate.

Original Text of Section V of the Twentieth Amendment to the Constitution of the United States

Sections I and II shall take effect on the 15th day of October following the ratification of this article.

Modern Text of Section V of the Twentieth Amendment to the Constitution of the United States

Sections I and II shall take effect on the 15th of October following the ratification of this article.

Original Text of Section VI of the Twentieth Amendment to the Constitution of the United States

This article shall be inoperative unless it shall have been ratified as an amendment to the Constitution by the legislatures of three-fourths of the several States within seven years from the date of its submission.

Modern Text of Section VI of the Twentieth Amendment to the Constitution of the United States

This article shall be inoperative unless it shall have been ratified as an amendment to the Constitution by the legislatures of three-fourths of the several States within seven years from the date of its submission.

Discussion

This Amendment is what we decided to call a "lawyer what if." It basically says what you do if there is no President Elect (or VP Elect). It also defines some swearing in dates. It is not controversial in any way and most people probably aren't even aware it is in the document. So consider yourself one of the few! Congratulations!

Chapter 29

Amendment XXI

Note: Passed by Congress February 20, 1933. Ratified December 5, 1933.

Original Text of Section I of the Twenty First Amendment to the Constitution of the United States

The eighteenth article of amendment to the Constitution of the United States is hereby repealed.

Modern Text of Section I of the Twenty First Amendment to the Constitution of the United States

The 18th amendment to the Constitution is removed or invalidated.

Original Text of Section II of the Twenty First Amendment to the Constitution of the United States

The transportation or importation into any State, Territory, or Possession of the United States for delivery or use therein of intoxicating liquors, in violation of the laws thereof, is hereby prohibited.

Modern Text of Section II of the Twenty First Amendment to the Constitution of the United States

Transporting or importing alcohol into any State or Territory of the United States in which a local government has created a law against alcohol, is still illegal.

Original Text of Section III of the Twenty First

Amendment to the Constitution of the United States

This article shall be inoperative unless it shall have been ratified as an amendment to the Constitution by conventions in the several States, as provided in the Constitution, within seven years from the date of the submission hereof to the States by the Congress.

Modern Text of Section III of the Twenty First Amendment to the Constitution of the United States

This article will be not be used unless accepted as part of the Constitution within seven years of the date it was submitted to congress.

Discussion

The amendment merely took the Eighteenth Amendment and put it where it belonged in the first place. Throw that sucker out, burn it, use it for target practice for people exercising rights under the Second Amendment. This returned the rights to make decisions on alcoholic beverages back to the States or localities.

What fun would Super Bowl Sunday be, if we weren't allowed to have a beer?

Chapter 30

Amendment XXII

Note: Passed by Congress March 21, 1947. Ratified February 27, 1951.

Original Text of Section I of the Twenty Second Amendment to the Constitution of the United States

No person shall be elected to the office of the President more than twice, and no person who has held the office of President, or acted as President, for more than two years of a term to which some other person was elected President shall be elected to the office of President more than once. But this Article shall not apply to any person holding the office of President when this Article was proposed by Congress, and shall not prevent any person who may be holding the office of President, or acting as President, during the term within which this Article becomes operative from holding the office of President or acting as President during the remainder of such term.

Modern Text of Section I of the Twenty Second Amendment to the Constitution of the United States

No person can hold the office of President more than twice.

No person who has be in office as President for more than two years of a term of another elected President can hold the elected office of President more than once.

This amendment will not affect any standing person holding the office of President or acting as the office of President during the remainder of their term.

Original Text of Section II of the Twenty Second Amendment to the Constitution of the United States

This article shall be inoperative unless it shall have been ratified as an amendment to the Constitution by the legislatures of three-fourths of the several States within seven years from the date of its submission to the States by the Congress.

Modern Text of Section II of the Twenty Second Amendment to the Constitution of the United States

This will not go into affect unless accepted by three-fourths vote of congress within seven years from the date of submission.

Discussion

This Amendment set a term limit for Presidents. There is only one President to ever serve more than that. Prior to this passing the remainder either term limited themselves, or for whatever reason (impending electoral loss?) did not serve more than two.

We think that someone serving in that Office for too long would start to get delusions or feelings of nobility and certainly would not be connected with problems facing the majority of Americans.

Term Limits for Presidents are a good thing, at least in our humble opinion. There is no reason someone who has been President twice can't still stay involved in our political process and influence policy. They still have Constitutional rights to do so. These ex-Presidents could even run for Senate (it has happened before). In short, eight years in the Oval Office is enough. Move on and do something else after that.

Now if only we had the same thing for Senators and Representatives. Perhaps someday we will get that Amendment added to the Constitution.

Chapter 31

Amendment XXIII

Note: Passed by Congress June 16, 1960. Ratified March 29, 1961.

Original Text of Section I of the Twenty Third Amendment to the Constitution of the United States

The District constituting the seat of Government of the United States shall appoint in such manner as Congress may direct:

A number of electors of President and Vice President equal to the whole number of Senators and Representatives in Congress to which the District would be entitled if it were a State, but in no event more than the least populous State; they shall be in addition to those appointed by the States, but they shall be considered, for the purposes of the election of President and Vice President, to be electors appointed by a State; and they shall meet in the District and perform such duties as provided by the twelfth article of amendment.

Modern Text of Section I of the Twenty Third Amendment to the Constitution of the United States

Congress decides where the Capital (The District of Columbia) of the United States will be.

The District of Columbia will be granted the same number of electors as the least populace state within the United States for the purpose of voting for the office of President and Vice President.

Those electors shall meet in the District and do their job as stated in the Twelfth Amendment.

Original Text of Section II of the Twenty Third Amendment to the Constitution of the United States

The Congress shall have power to enforce this article by appropriate legislation.

Modern Text of Section II of the Twenty Third Amendment to the Constitution of the United States

Congress will enforce this law.

Discussion

This really non-issue amendment just gives the residents of Washington DC a say in who is President. Up to the time this Amendment was ratified they could not vote for the President or Vice President in a way that counted.

It is great that this happened or the residents there (who aren't technically in a State) would have no say at all in the highest levels of elected leadership of this great Nation.

Chapter 32
Amendment XXIV

Note: Passed by Congress August 27, 1962. Ratified January 23, 1964.

Original Text of Section I of the Twenty Fourth Amendment to the Constitution of the United States

The right of citizens of the United States to vote in any primary or other election for President or Vice President, for electors for President or Vice President, or for Senator or Representative in Congress, shall not be denied or abridged by the United States or any State by reason of failure to pay any poll tax or other tax.

Modern Text of Section I of the Twenty Fourth Amendment to the Constitution of the United States

There will be no fee, cost or tax for the right to vote as a citizen in an election of the United States for the office or President, Vice President, or members of both houses of Congress.

Original Text of Section II of the Twenty Fourth Amendment to the Constitution of the United States

The Congress shall have power to enforce this article by appropriate legislation.

Modern Text of Section II of the Twenty Fourth Amendment to the Constitution of the United States

Congress will enforce this law.

Discussion

In the Southern United States there were a variety of tricks to keep African Americans from voting. These had existed since the end of slavery.

The most widespread trick was a poll tax (or fee, it was advertised and enforced in a variety of ways).

The way it would work is someone claiming to be a poll worker would stand outside the polling location and see who was coming to vote and charge a "tax".

In theory it would apply to everyone.

In practice many poll tax collectors wouldn't see the white people. As a result of that this Amendment was put into the Constitution ending the practice.

Personally we want a time machine so we can go back and beat the snot out of whoever put this practice in place to begin with. It should have never happened.

Gladly we have a method of fixing these problems in the Country and we did.

Chapter 33

Amendment XXV

Note: Passed by Congress July 6, 1965. Ratified February 10, 1967.

Original Text of Section I of the Twenty Fifth Amendment to the Constitution of the United States

In case of the removal of the President from office or of his death or resignation, the Vice President shall become President.

Modern Text of Section I of the Twenty Fifth Amendment to the Constitution of the United States

The Vice President will become President if the current President dies in office, resigns or is impeached and removed.

Original Text of Section II of the Twenty Fifth Amendment to the Constitution of the United States

Whenever there is a vacancy in the office of the Vice President, the President shall nominate a Vice President who shall take office upon confirmation by a majority vote of both Houses of Congress.

Modern Text of Section II of the Twenty Fifth Amendment to the Constitution of the United States

In the event of a vacancy the President can select a new Vice President who, on a majority vote from both houses of Congress, takes that office.

Original Text of Section III of the Twenty Fifth Amendment to the Constitution of the United States

Whenever the President transmits to the President pro tempore of the Senate and the Speaker of the House of Representatives his written declaration that he is unable to discharge the powers and duties of his office, and until he transmits to them a written declaration to the contrary, such powers and duties shall be discharged by the Vice President as Acting President.

Modern Text of Section III of the Twenty Fifth Amendment to the Constitution of the United States

When the sitting President has sent to the leaders of both houses of Congress his or her written declaration that he or she is unable to act as President, the Vice President shall take over the duties of the office of President until the President sends a written letter to the leaders of Congress declaring his renewed ability to be the President.

Original Text of Section IV of the Twenty Fifth Amendment to the Constitution of the United States

Whenever the Vice President and a majority of either the principal officers of the executive departments or of such other body as Congress may by law provide, transmit to the President pro tempore of the Senate and the Speaker of the House of Representatives their written declaration that the President is unable to discharge the powers and duties of his office, the Vice President shall immediately assume the powers and duties of the office as Acting President.

Thereafter, when the President transmits to the

President pro tempore of the Senate and the Speaker of the House of Representatives his written declaration that no inability exists, he shall resume the powers and duties of his office unless the Vice President and a majority of either the principal officers of the executive department or of such other body as Congress may by law provide, transmit within four days to the President pro tempore of the Senate and the Speaker of the House of Representatives their written declaration that the President is unable to discharge the powers and duties of his office. Thereupon Congress shall decide the issue, assembling within forty-eight hours for that purpose if not in session. If the Congress, within twenty-one days after receipt of the latter written declaration, or, if Congress is not in session, within twenty-one days after Congress is required to assemble, determines by two-thirds vote of both Houses that the President is unable to discharge the powers and duties of his office, the Vice President shall continue to discharge the same as Acting President; otherwise, the President shall resume the powers and duties of his office.

Modern Text of Section IV of the Twenty Fifth Amendment to the Constitution of the United States

When the Vice President and other Leaders of the Executive departments can, by law, send their written declaration of the unfitness of the standing President. The Vice President shall take over the duties as acting President.

If and when the President sends the leaders of Congress his/her written statement that no inability exists, they resume the powers and duties of President, unless the Vice President and the other leaders of the Executive Departments send within four days their statement of the Presidents inability or discharge the duties and responsibilities of his office. Congress at this time will decide the issue, assembling within forty-eight hours for this purpose, if not in session. If Congress, within twenty-one days determines by a two-thirds majority vote of both houses the Presidents inability to perform their duties, the Vice President will continue on as Acting President. Otherwise, the President will once again take over the duties and responsibilities of his or her office.

Discussion

This Amendment is interesting. It is another game (somewhat based in an incident that happened) of legal "what iffery." Basically it outlines a series of Presidential succession steps in detail.

It also tells us that if we have a President who is unable to continue, that the Cabinet can take him out of office and elevate the Vice President.

Think about this Amendment in the context of modern medicine.

With modern medicine we can keep people alive for extended periods of time. This would, essentially, allow a President who suffered a stroke (for instance but certainly not limited to a stroke) to then be President while in no condition to do the job. This Amendment offers a legal method to go from one President to the next in line without causing a large amount of chaos in our highest leadership positions.

We like this as a "just in case" provision.

Chapter 34

Amendment XXVI

Note: Passed by Congress March 23, 1971. Ratified July 1, 1971.

Amendment 14, section 2, of the Constitution was modified by section 1 of the 26th amendment.

Original Text of Section I of the Twenty Sixth Amendment to the Constitution of the United States

The right of citizens of the United States, who are eighteen years of age or older, to vote shall not be denied or abridged by the United States or by any State on account of age.

Modern Text of Section I of the Twenty Sixth Amendment to the Constitution of the United States

Citizens of the United States who are eighteen years of age or older have the right to vote

Original Text of Section II of the Twenty Sixth Amendment to the Constitution of the United States

The Congress shall have power to enforce this article by appropriate legislation.

Modern Text of Section II of the Twenty Sixth Amendment to the Constitution of the United States

Congress will enforce this law.

Discussion

Prior to this some States had voting ages higher than eighteen. So...Let's think about this.

At eighteen you could be drafted, serve in the military, be tried as an adult in court, but not vote? Interesting.

This solved that problem.

However, we have some questions.

What about that drinking age thing?

Why is this not included?

You can do all these things that declare you as an adult but not adult enough to drink?

We need to seriously look at the definition of an adult in this country and either make everything twenty-one or lower the drinking age. Right now we sit both sides of this issue and it seems illogical to us. We are not advocating lowering the age perhaps the right answer is raising these other age requirements. However, one or the other should happen. There is an apparent mismatch in our definition of adult.

Chapter 35

Amendment XXVII

Note: Originally proposed Sept. 25, 1789. Ratified May 7, 1992.

Original Text of the Twenty Seventh Amendment to the Constitution of the United States

No law, varying the compensation for the services of the Senators and Representatives, shall take effect, until an election of representatives shall have intervened.

Modern Text of the Twenty Seventh Amendment to the Constitution of the United States

No pay raise for Senators and Representatives will take effect until the current term of office has ended.

Discussion

This Amendment is another housekeeping Amendment. Basically what would happened was that people would run for Congress...the first vote before them every term would be "should we all get a raise?"

Well...yeah sure why not.

Who would vote no to a personal pay raise?

What this did was say that Congress could vote pay raises for Congress because their salary is defined by law but no raise will take effect until the next session of Congress. Therefore whoever is in office NEXT time will get the raise.

Make your own decision on what you think about this but we think it is an important safeguard of tax dollars.

The really interesting bit to us is the Proposed Date of this Amendment versus the Ratification Date. This one took the elected officials a while to decide this was a good idea.

We the people really had to get after them in order for this to happen. We really need to watch what our elected leaders are doing with our money and our laws. The moment we disengage will be the moment that someone in office decides to take advantage of our goodwill.

Appendix A
Signers of the US Constitution

Virginia

1 - George Washington
2 - John Blair
3 - James Madison

South Carolina

4 - Pierce Butler South Carolina
5 - Charles Pinckney South Carolina
6 - John Rutledge South Carolina
7 - Charles Cotesworth Pinckney South Carolina

Pennsylvania

8 - George Clymer
9 - Thomas Fitzsimons
10 - Benjamin Franklin
11 - Jared Ingersoll
12 - Thomas Mifflin
13 - Gouverneur Morris
14 - Robert Morris
15 - James Wilson

New Jersey

16 - David Brearley

17 - Jonathan Dayton
18 - William Livingston
19 - William Paterson

New York

20 - Alexander Hamilton

North Carolina

21 - William Blount
22 - Richard D. Spaight
23 - Hugh Williamson

Connecticut

24 - William S. Johnson Connecticut
25 - Roger Sherman Connecticut

Delaware

26 - Richard Bassett
27 - Gunning Bedford, Jr
28 - Jacob Broom
29 - John Dickinson
30 - George Read

Georgia

31 - Abraham Baldwin
32 - William Few

Maryland

33 - Daniel Carroll
34 - Daniel Jenifer
35 - James McHenry

Massachusetts

36 - Rufus King
37 - Nathaniel Gorham

New Hampshire

38 - Nicholas Gilman
39 - John Langdon

Secretary of the Constitutional Convention

40 – William Jackson

Appendix B

Original Text of the United States Constitution

Preamble

We the People of the United States, in Order to form a more perfect Union, establish Justice, insure domestic Tranquility, provide for the common defence, promote the general Welfare, and secure the Blessings of Liberty to ourselves and our Posterity, do ordain and establish this Constitution for the United States of America.

Article I

Section I

All legislative Powers herein granted shall be vested in a Congress of the United States, which shall consist of a Senate and House of Representatives.

Section II

The House of Representatives shall be composed of Members chosen every second Year by the People of the several States, and the Electors in each State shall have the Qualifications requisite for Electors of the most numerous Branch of the State Legislature.

No Person shall be a Representative who shall not have attained to the Age of twenty five Years, and been seven Years a Citizen of the United States, and who shall not, when elected, be an Inhabitant of that State in which he shall be chosen.

Representatives and direct Taxes shall be apportioned

among the several States which may be included within this Union, according to their respective Numbers, which shall be determined by adding to the whole Number of free Persons, including those bound to Service for a Term of Years, and excluding Indians not taxed, three fifths of all other Persons. The actual Enumeration shall be made within three Years after the first Meeting of the Congress of the United States, and within every subsequent Term of ten Years, in such Manner as they shall by Law direct. The Number of Representatives shall not exceed one for every thirty Thousand, but each State shall have at Least one Representative; and until such enumeration shall be made, the State of New Hampshire shall be entitled to chuse three, Massachusetts eight, Rhode-Island and Providence Plantations one, Connecticut five, New-York six, New Jersey four, Pennsylvania eight, Delaware one, Maryland six, Virginia ten, North Carolina five, South Carolina five, and Georgia three.

When vacancies happen in the Representation from any State, the Executive Authority thereof shall issue Writs of Election to fill such Vacancies.

The House of Representatives shall chuse their Speaker and other Officers; and shall have the sole Power of Impeachment.

Section III

The Senate of the United States shall be composed of two Senators from each State, chosen by the Legislature thereof for six Years; and each Senator shall have one Vote.

Immediately after they shall be assembled in Consequence of the first Election, they shall be divided as equally as may be into three Classes. The Seats of the Senators of the first Class shall be vacated at the Expiration of the second Year, of the second Class at the Expiration of the fourth Year, and of the third Class at the Expiration of the sixth Year, so that one third may be chosen every second Year;

and if Vacancies happen by Resignation, or otherwise, during the Recess of the Legislature of any State, the Executive thereof may make temporary Appointments until the next Meeting of the Legislature, which shall then fill such Vacancies.

No Person shall be a Senator who shall not have attained to the Age of thirty Years, and been nine Years a Citizen of the United States, and who shall not, when elected, be an Inhabitant of that State for which he shall be chosen.

The Vice President of the United States shall be President of the Senate, but shall have no Vote, unless they be equally divided.

The Senate shall chuse their other Officers, and also a President pro tempore, in the Absence of the Vice President, or when he shall exercise the Office of President of the United States.

The Senate shall have the sole Power to try all Impeachments. When sitting for that Purpose, they shall be on Oath or Affirmation. When the President of the United States is tried, the Chief Justice shall preside: And no Person shall be convicted without the Concurrence of two thirds of the Members present.

Judgment in Cases of Impeachment shall not extend further than to removal from Office, and disqualification to hold and enjoy any Office of honor, Trust or Profit under the United States: but the Party convicted shall nevertheless be liable and subject to Indictment, Trial, Judgment and Punishment, according to Law.

Section IV

The Times, Places and Manner of holding Elections for Senators and Representatives, shall be prescribed in each State by the Legislature thereof; but the Congress may at any time by Law make or alter such Regulations, except as to the Places of chusing Senators.

The Congress shall assemble at least once in every Year, and such Meeting shall be on the first Monday in December, unless they shall by Law appoint a different Day.

Section V

Each House shall be the Judge of the Elections, Returns and Qualifications of its own Members, and a Majority of each shall constitute a Quorum to do Business; but a smaller Number may adjourn from day to day, and may be authorized to compel the Attendance of absent Members, in such Manner, and under such Penalties as each House may provide.

Each House may determine the Rules of its Proceedings, punish its Members for disorderly Behaviour, and, with the Concurrence of two thirds, expel a Member.

Each House shall keep a Journal of its Proceedings, and from time to time publish the same, excepting such Parts as may in their Judgment require Secrecy; and the Yeas and Nays of the Members of either House on any question shall, at the Desire of one fifth of those Present, be entered on the Journal.

Neither House, during the Session of Congress, shall, without the Consent of the other, adjourn for more than three days, nor to any other Place than that in which the two Houses shall be sitting.

Section VI

The Senators and Representatives shall receive a Compensation for their Services, to be ascertained by Law, and paid out of the Treasury of the United States. They shall in all Cases, except Treason, Felony and Breach of the Peace, be privileged from Arrest during their Attendance at the Session of their respective Houses, and in going to and returning from the same; and for any Speech or Debate in either House, they shall not be questioned in any other Place.

No Senator or Representative shall, during the Time for which he was elected, be appointed to any civil Office under the Authority of the United States, which shall have been created, or the Emoluments whereof shall have been encreased during such time; and no Person holding any Office under the United States, shall be a Member of either House during his Continuance in Office.

Section VII

All Bills for raising Revenue shall originate in the House of Representatives; but the Senate may propose or concur with Amendments as on other Bills.

Every Bill which shall have passed the House of Representatives and the Senate, shall, before it become a Law, be presented to the President of the United States: If he approve he shall sign it, but if not he shall return it, with his Objections to that House in which it shall have originated, who shall enter the Objections at large on their Journal, and proceed to reconsider it. If after such Reconsideration two thirds of that House shall agree to pass the Bill, it shall be sent, together with the Objections, to the other House, by which it shall likewise be reconsidered, and if approved by two thirds of that House, it shall become a Law. But in all such Cases the Votes of both Houses shall be determined by yeas and Nays, and the Names of the Persons voting for and against the Bill shall be entered on the Journal of each House respectively. If any Bill shall not be returned by the President within ten Days (Sundays excepted) after it shall have been presented to him, the Same shall be a Law, in like Manner as if he had signed it, unless the Congress by their Adjournment prevent its Return, in which Case it shall not be a Law.

Every Order, Resolution, or Vote to which the Concurrence of the Senate and House of Representatives may be necessary (except on a question of Adjournment) shall be presented to the President of the United States; and before the Same shall take Effect, shall be approved by him, or being disapproved by him, shall be repassed by two thirds of the Senate and House of Representatives, according to the Rules and Limitations prescribed in the Case of a Bill.

Section VIII

The Congress shall have Power To lay and collect Taxes, Duties, Imposts and Excises, to pay the Debts and provide for the common Defence and general Welfare of the United States; but all Duties, Imposts and Excises shall be uniform throughout the United States;

To borrow Money on the credit of the United States;

To regulate Commerce with foreign Nations, and among the several States, and with the Indian Tribes;

To establish an uniform Rule of Naturalization, and uniform Laws on the subject of Bankruptcies throughout the United States;

To coin Money, regulate the Value thereof, and of foreign Coin, and fix the Standard of Weights and Measures;

To provide for the Punishment of counterfeiting the Securities and current Coin of the United States;

To establish Post Offices and post Roads;

To promote the Progress of Science and useful Arts, by securing for limited Times to Authors and Inventors the exclusive Right to their respective Writings and Discoveries;

To constitute Tribunals inferior to the supreme Court;

To define and punish Piracies and Felonies committed on the high Seas, and Offences against the Law of Nations;

To declare War, grant Letters of Marque and Reprisal, and

make Rules concerning Captures on Land and Water;

To raise and support Armies, but no Appropriation of Money to that Use shall be for a longer Term than two Years;

To provide and maintain a Navy;

To make Rules for the Government and Regulation of the land and naval Forces;

To provide for calling forth the Militia to execute the Laws of the Union, suppress Insurrections and repel Invasions;

To provide for organizing, arming, and disciplining, the Militia, and for governing such Part of them as may be employed in the Service of the United States, reserving to the States respectively, the Appointment of the Officers, and the Authority of training the Militia according to the discipline prescribed by Congress;

To exercise exclusive Legislation in all Cases whatsoever, over such District (not exceeding ten Miles square) as may, by Cession of particular States, and the Acceptance of Congress, become the Seat of the Government of the United States, and to exercise like Authority over all Places purchased by the Consent of the Legislature of the State in which the Same shall be, for the Erection of Forts, Magazines, Arsenals, dock-Yards, and other needful Buildings;--And

To make all Laws which shall be necessary and proper for carrying into Execution the foregoing Powers, and all other Powers vested by this Constitution in the Government of the United States, or in any Department or Officer thereof.

Section IX

The Migration or Importation of such Persons as any of the States now existing shall think proper to admit, shall not be prohibited by the Congress prior to the Year one thousand eight hundred and eight, but a Tax or duty may be imposed on such Importation, not exceeding ten dollars for each Person.

The Privilege of the Writ of Habeas Corpus shall not be suspended, unless when in Cases of Rebellion or Invasion the public Safety may require it.

No Bill of Attainder or ex post facto Law shall be passed.

No Capitation, or other direct, Tax shall be laid, unless in Proportion to the Census or enumeration herein before directed to be taken.

No Tax or Duty shall be laid on Articles exported from any State.

No Preference shall be given by any Regulation of Commerce or Revenue to the Ports of one State over those of another; nor shall Vessels bound to, or from, one State, be obliged to enter, clear, or pay Duties in another.

No Money shall be drawn from the Treasury, but in Consequence of Appropriations made by Law; and a regular Statement and Account of the Receipts and Expenditures of all public Money shall be published from time to time.

No Title of Nobility shall be granted by the United States: And no Person holding any Office of Profit or Trust under them, shall, without the Consent of the Congress, accept of any present, Emolument, Office, or Title, of any kind whatever, from any King, Prince, or foreign State.

Section X

No State shall enter into any Treaty, Alliance, or Confederation; grant Letters of Marque and Reprisal; coin Money; emit Bills of Credit; make any Thing but gold and silver Coin a Tender in Payment of Debts; pass any Bill of Attainder, ex post facto Law, or Law impairing the Obligation of Contracts, or grant any Title of Nobility.

No State shall, without the Consent of the Congress, lay any Imposts or Duties on Imports or Exports, except what may be absolutely necessary for executing it's inspection Laws: and the net Produce of all Duties and Imposts, laid by any State on Imports or Exports, shall be for the Use of the Treasury of the United States; and all such Laws shall be subject to the Revision and Controul of the Congress.

No State shall, without the Consent of Congress, lay any Duty of Tonnage, keep Troops, or Ships of War in time of Peace, enter into any Agreement or Compact with another State, or with a foreign Power, or engage in War, unless actually invaded, or in such imminent Danger as will not admit of delay.

Article II

Section I

The executive Power shall be vested in a President of the United States of America. He shall hold his Office during the Term of four Years, and, together with the Vice President, chosen for the same Term, be elected, as follows:

Each State shall appoint, in such Manner as the Legislature thereof may direct, a Number of Electors, equal to the whole Number of Senators and Representatives to which the State may be entitled in the Congress: but no Senator or Representative, or Person holding an Office of Trust or Profit under the United States, shall be appointed an Elector.

The Electors shall meet in their respective States, and vote by Ballot for two Persons, of whom one at least shall not be an Inhabitant of the same State with themselves. And they shall make a List of all the Persons voted for, and of the Number of Votes for each; which List they shall sign and certify, and transmit sealed to the Seat of the Government of the United States, directed to the President of the Senate. The President of the Senate shall, in the Presence of the Senate and House of Representatives, open all the Certificates, and the Votes shall then be counted. The Person having the greatest Number of Votes shall be the President, if such Number be a Majority of the whole Number of Electors appointed; and if there be more than one who have such Majority, and have an equal Number of Votes, then the House of Representatives shall immediately chuse by Ballot one of them for President; and if no Person have a Majority, then from the five highest on the List the said House shall in like Manner chuse the President. But in chusing the President, the Votes shall be taken by States, the Representation from each State having one Vote; A quorum for this purpose shall consist of a Member or Members from two thirds of the States, and a Majority of all the States shall be necessary to a Choice. In every Case, after the Choice of the President, the Person having the greatest Number of Votes of the Electors shall be the Vice President. But if there should remain two or more who have equal Votes, the Senate shall chuse from them by Ballot the Vice President.

The Congress may determine the Time of chusing the Electors, and the Day on which they shall give their Votes; which Day shall be the same throughout the United States.

No Person except a natural born Citizen, or a Citizen of the United States, at the time of the Adoption of this Constitution, shall be eligible to the Office of President; neither shall any Person be eligible to that Office who shall not have attained to the Age of thirty five Years, and been fourteen Years a Resident within the United States.

In Case of the Removal of the President from Office, or of his Death, Resignation, or Inability to discharge the Powers and Duties of the said Office, the Same shall devolve on the Vice President, and the Congress may by Law provide for the Case of Removal, Death, Resignation or Inability, both of the President and Vice President, declaring what Officer shall then act as President, and such Officer shall act accordingly, until the Disability be removed, or a President shall be elected.

The President shall, at stated Times, receive for his Services, a Compensation, which shall neither be increased nor diminished during the Period for which he shall have been elected, and he shall not receive within that Period any other Emolument from the United States, or any of them.

Before he enter on the Execution of his Office, he shall take the following Oath or Affirmation:--"I do solemnly swear (or affirm) that I will faithfully execute the Office of President of the United States, and will to the best of my Ability, preserve, protect and defend the Constitution of the United States."

Section II

The President shall be Commander in Chief of the Army and Navy of the United States, and of the Militia of the several States, when called into the actual Service of the United States; he may require the Opinion, in writing, of the principal Officer in each of the executive Departments, upon any Subject relating to the Duties of their respective Offices, and he shall have Power to grant Reprieves and Pardons for Offences against the United States, except in Cases of Impeachment.

He shall have Power, by and with the Advice and Consent of the Senate, to make Treaties, provided two thirds of the Senators present concur; and he shall nominate, and by and with the Advice and Consent of the Senate, shall appoint Ambassadors, other public Ministers and Consuls, Judges of the supreme Court, and all other Officers of the United States, whose Appointments are not herein otherwise provided for, and which shall be established by Law: but the Congress may by Law vest the Appointment of such inferior Officers, as they think proper, in the President alone, in the Courts of Law, or in the Heads of Departments.

The President shall have Power to fill up all Vacancies that may happen during the Recess of the Senate, by granting Commissions which shall expire at the End of their next Session.

Section III

He shall from time to time give to the Congress Information of the State of the Union, and recommend to their Consideration such Measures as he shall judge necessary and expedient; he may, on extraordinary Occasions, convene both Houses, or either of them, and in Case of Disagreement between them, with Respect to the Time of Adjournment, he may adjourn them to such Time as he shall think proper; he shall receive Ambassadors and other public Ministers; he shall take Care that the Laws be faithfully executed, and shall Commission all the Officers of the United States.

Section IV

The President, Vice President and all civil Officers of the United States, shall be removed from Office on Impeachment for, and Conviction of, Treason, Bribery, or other high Crimes and Misdemeanors.

Article III

Section I

The judicial Power of the United States shall be vested in one supreme Court, and in such inferior Courts as the Congress may from time to time ordain and establish. The Judges, both of the supreme and inferior Courts, shall hold their Offices during good Behaviour, and shall, at stated Times, receive for their Services a Compensation, which shall not be diminished during their Continuance in

Office.

Section II

The judicial Power shall extend to all Cases, in Law and Equity, arising under this Constitution, the Laws of the United States, and Treaties made, or which shall be made, under their Authority;--to all Cases affecting Ambassadors, other public Ministers and Consuls;--to all Cases of admiralty and maritime Jurisdiction;--to Controversies to which the United States shall be a Party;-- to Controversies between two or more States;-- between a State and Citizens of another State,--between Citizens of different States,--between Citizens of the same State claiming Lands under Grants of different States, and between a State, or the Citizens thereof, and foreign States, Citizens or Subjects.

In all Cases affecting Ambassadors, other public Ministers and Consuls, and those in which a State shall be Party, the supreme Court shall have original Jurisdiction. In all the other Cases before mentioned, the supreme Court shall have appellate Jurisdiction, both as to Law and Fact, with such Exceptions, and under such Regulations as the Congress shall make.

The Trial of all Crimes, except in Cases of Impeachment, shall be by Jury; and such Trial shall be held in the State where the said Crimes shall have been committed; but when not committed within any State, the Trial shall be at such Place or Places as the Congress may by Law have directed.

Section III

Treason against the United States, shall consist only in levying War against them, or in adhering to their Enemies, giving them Aid and Comfort. No Person shall be convicted of Treason unless on the Testimony of two Witnesses to the same overt Act, or on Confession in open

Court.

The Congress shall have Power to declare the Punishment of Treason, but no Attainder of Treason shall work Corruption of Blood, or Forfeiture except during the Life of the Person attainted.

Article IV

Section I

Full Faith and Credit shall be given in each State to the public Acts, Records, and judicial Proceedings of every other State. And the Congress may by general Laws prescribe the Manner in which such Acts, Records and Proceedings shall be proved, and the Effect thereof.

Section II

The Citizens of each State shall be entitled to all Privileges and Immunities of Citizens in the several States.

A Person charged in any State with Treason, Felony, or other Crime, who shall flee from Justice, and be found in another State, shall on Demand of the executive Authority of the State from which he fled, be delivered up, to be removed to the State having Jurisdiction of the Crime.

No Person held to Service or Labour in one State, under the Laws thereof, escaping into another, shall, in Consequence of any Law or Regulation therein, be discharged from such Service or Labour, but shall be delivered up on Claim of the Party to whom such Service or Labour may be due.

Section III

New States may be admitted by the Congress into this Union; but no new State shall be formed or erected within the Jurisdiction of any other State; nor any State be formed by the Junction of two or more States, or Parts of States, without the Consent of the Legislatures of the States concerned as well as of the Congress.

The Congress shall have Power to dispose of and make all needful Rules and Regulations respecting the Territory or other Property belonging to the United States; and nothing in this Constitution shall be so construed as to Prejudice any Claims of the United States, or of any particular State.

Section IV

The United States shall guarantee to every State in this Union a Republican Form of Government, and shall protect each of them against Invasion; and on Application of the Legislature, or of the Executive (when the Legislature cannot be convened), against domestic Violence.

Article V

The Congress, whenever two thirds of both Houses shall deem it necessary, shall propose Amendments to this Constitution, or, on the Application of the Legislatures of two thirds of the several States, shall call a Convention for proposing Amendments, which, in either Case, shall be valid to all Intents and Purposes, as Part of this Constitution, when ratified by the Legislatures of three fourths of the several States, or by Conventions in three fourths thereof, as the one or the other Mode of Ratification may be proposed by the Congress; Provided that no Amendment which may be made prior to the Year One thousand eight hundred and eight shall in any Manner affect the first and fourth Clauses in the Ninth Section of the first Article; and that no State, without its Consent, shall be deprived of its equal Suffrage in the Senate.

Article VI

All Debts contracted and Engagements entered into, before the Adoption of this Constitution, shall be as valid against the United States under this Constitution, as under the Confederation.

This Constitution, and the Laws of the United States which shall be made in Pursuance thereof; and all Treaties made, or which shall be made, under the Authority of the United States, shall be the supreme Law of the Land; and the Judges in every State shall be bound thereby, any Thing in the Constitution or Laws of any State to the Contrary notwithstanding.

The Senators and Representatives before mentioned, and the Members of the several State Legislatures, and all executive and judicial Officers, both of the United States and of the several States, shall be bound by Oath or Affirmation, to support this Constitution; but no religious Test shall ever be required as a Qualification to any Office or public Trust under the United States.

Article VII

The Ratification of the Conventions of nine States, shall be sufficient for the Establishment of this Constitution between the States so ratifying the Same.

The Word, "the," being interlined between the seventh and eighth Lines of the first Page, the Word "Thirty" being partly written on an Erazure in the fifteenth Line of the first Page, The Words "is tried" being interlined between the thirty second and thirty third Lines of the first Page and the Word "the" being interlined between the forty third and forty fourth Lines of the second Page.

Attest William Jackson Secretary

done in Convention by the Unanimous Consent of the States present the Seventeenth Day of September in the Year of our Lord one thousand seven hundred and Eighty seven and of the Independance of the United States of America the Twelfth In witness whereof We have hereunto subscribed our Names,

Amendment I

Congress shall make no law respecting an establishment of religion, or prohibiting the free exercise thereof; or abridging the freedom of speech, or of the press; or the right of the people peaceably to assemble, and to petition the Government for a redress of grievances.

Amendment II

A well-regulated Militia, being necessary to the security of a free State, the right of the people to keep and bear Arms, shall not be infringed.

Amendment III

No Soldier shall, in time of peace be quartered in any house, without the consent of the Owner, nor in time of war, but in a manner to be prescribed by law.

Amendment IV

The right of the people to be secure in their persons, houses, papers, and effects, against unreasonable searches and seizures, shall not be violated, and no Warrants shall issue, but upon probable cause, supported by Oath or affirmation, and particularly describing the place to be searched, and the persons or things to be seized.

Amendment V

No person shall be held to answer for a capital, or otherwise infamous crime, unless on a presentment or indictment of a Grand Jury, except in cases arising in the land or naval forces, or in the Militia, when in actual service in time of War or public danger; nor shall any person be subject for the same offence to be twice put in jeopardy of life or limb; nor shall be compelled in any criminal case to be a witness against himself, nor be deprived of life, liberty, or property, without due process of law; nor shall private property be taken for public use, without just compensation.

Amendment VI

In all criminal prosecutions, the accused shall enjoy the right to a speedy and public trial, by an impartial jury of the State and district wherein the crime shall have been committed, which district shall have been previously ascertained by law, and to be informed of the nature and cause of the accusation; to be confronted with the witnesses against him; to have compulsory process for obtaining witnesses in his favor, and to have the Assistance of Counsel for his defence.

Amendment VII

In Suits at common law, where the value in controversy shall exceed twenty dollars, the right of trial by jury shall be preserved, and no fact tried by a jury, shall be otherwise re-examined in any Court of the United States, than according to the rules of the common law.

Amendment VIII

Excessive bail shall not be required, nor excessive fines imposed, nor cruel and unusual punishments inflicted.

Amendment IX

The enumeration in the Constitution, of certain rights, shall not be construed to deny or disparage others retained by the people.

Amendment X

The powers not delegated to the United States by the Constitution, nor prohibited by it to the States, are reserved to the States respectively, or to the people.

Amendment XI

The Judicial power of the United States shall not be construed to extend to any suit in law or equity, commenced or prosecuted against one of the United States by Citizens of another State, or by Citizens or Subjects of any Foreign State.

Amendment XII

The Electors shall meet in their respective states and vote by ballot for President and Vice-President, one of whom, at least, shall not be an inhabitant of the same state with themselves; they shall name in their ballots the person voted for as President, and in distinct ballots the person voted for as Vice-President, and they shall make distinct lists of all persons voted for as President, and of all persons voted for as Vice-President, and of the number of votes for each, which lists they shall sign and certify, and transmit sealed to the seat of the government of the United States, directed to the President of the Senate; -- the President of the Senate shall, in the presence of the Senate and House of Representatives, open all the certificates and the votes shall then be counted; -- The person having the greatest number of votes for President, shall be the President, if such number be a majority of the whole number of Electors appointed; and if no person have such majority, then from the persons having the highest numbers not exceeding three on the list of those voted for as President, the House of Representatives shall choose immediately, by ballot, the President. But in choosing the President, the votes shall be taken by states, the representation from each state having one vote; a quorum for this purpose shall consist of a member or members from two-thirds of the states, and a majority of all the states shall be necessary to a choice. [And if the House of Representatives shall not choose a President whenever the right of choice shall devolve upon them, before the fourth day of March next following, then the Vice-President shall act as President, as in case of the death or other constitutional disability of the President. --]* The person having the greatest number of votes as Vice-President, shall be the Vice-President, if such number be a majority of the whole number of Electors appointed, and if no person have a majority, then from the two highest numbers on the list, the Senate shall choose the Vice-President; a quorum for the purpose shall consist of two-thirds of the whole number of Senators, and a majority of the whole number shall be necessary to a choice. But no person constitutionally ineligible to the office of President shall be eligible to that of Vice-President of the United States.

Amendment XIII

Section I

Neither slavery nor involuntary servitude, except as a punishment for crime whereof the party shall have been duly convicted, shall exist within the United States, or any place subject to their jurisdiction.

Section II

Congress shall have power to enforce this article by appropriate legislation.

Amendment XIV

Section I

All persons born or naturalized in the United States, and subject to the jurisdiction thereof, are citizens of the United States and of the State wherein they reside. No State shall make or enforce any law which shall abridge the privileges or immunities of citizens of the United States; nor shall any State deprive any person of life, liberty, or property, without due process of law; nor deny to any person within its jurisdiction the equal protection of the laws.

Section II

Representatives shall be apportioned among the several States according to their respective numbers, counting the whole number of persons in each State, excluding Indians not taxed. But when the right to vote at any election for the choice of electors for President and Vice-President of the United States, Representatives in Congress, the Executive and Judicial officers of a State, or the members of the

Legislature thereof, is denied to any of the male inhabitants of such State, being twenty-one years of age,* and citizens of the United States, or in any way abridged, except for participation in rebellion, or other crime, the basis of representation therein shall be reduced in the proportion which the number of such male citizens shall bear to the whole number of male citizens twenty-one years of age in such State.

Section III

No person shall be a Senator or Representative in Congress, or elector of President and Vice-President, or hold any office, civil or military, under the United States, or under any State, who, having previously taken an oath, as a member of Congress, or as an officer of the United States, or as a member of any State legislature, or as an executive or judicial officer of any State, to support the Constitution of the United States, shall have engaged in insurrection or rebellion against the same, or given aid or comfort to the enemies thereof. But Congress may by a vote of two-thirds of each House, remove such disability.

Section IV

The validity of the public debt of the United States, authorized by law, including debts incurred for payment of pensions and bounties for services in suppressing insurrection or rebellion, shall not be questioned. But neither the United States nor any State shall assume or pay any debt or obligation incurred in aid of insurrection or rebellion against the United States, or any claim for the loss or emancipation of any slave; but all such debts, obligations and claims shall be held illegal and void.

Section V

The Congress shall have the power to enforce, by appropriate legislation, the provisions of this article.

Amendment XV

Section I

The right of citizens of the United States to vote shall not be denied or abridged by the United States or by any State on account of race, color, or previous condition of servitude—

Section II

The Congress shall have the power to enforce this article by appropriate legislation.

Amendment XVI

The Congress shall have power to lay and collect taxes on incomes, from whatever source derived, without apportionment among the several States, and without regard to any census or enumeration.

Amendment XVII

The Senate of the United States shall be composed of two Senators from each State, elected by the people thereof, for six years; and each Senator shall have one vote. The electors in each State shall have the qualifications requisite for electors of the most numerous branch of the State legislatures.

When vacancies happen in the representation of any State in the Senate, the executive authority of such State shall issue writs of election to fill such vacancies: Provided, That the legislature of any State may empower the executive thereof to make temporary appointments until the people fill the vacancies by election as the legislature may direct.

This amendment shall not be so construed as to affect the election or term of any Senator chosen before it becomes valid as part of the Constitution.

Amendment XVIII

Section I

After one year from the ratification of this article the

manufacture, sale, or transportation of intoxicating liquors within, the importation thereof into, or the exportation thereof from the United States and all territory subject to the jurisdiction thereof for beverage purposes is hereby prohibited.

Section II

The Congress and the several States shall have concurrent power to enforce this article by appropriate legislation.

Section III

This article shall be inoperative unless it shall have been ratified as an amendment to the Constitution by the legislatures of the several States, as provided in the Constitution, within seven years from the date of the submission hereof to the States by the Congress.

Amendment XIX

The right of citizens of the United States to vote shall not be denied or abridged by the United States or by any State on account of sex.

Congress shall have power to enforce this article by appropriate legislation.

Amendment XX

Section I

The terms of the President and the Vice President shall end at noon on the 20th day of January, and the terms of Senators and Representatives at noon on the 3rd day of January, of the years in which such terms would have ended if this article had not been ratified; and the terms of their successors shall then begin.

Section II

The Congress shall assemble at least once in every year, and such meeting shall begin at noon on the 3d day of January, unless they shall by law appoint a different day.

Section III

If, at the time fixed for the beginning of the term of the President, the President elect shall have died, the Vice President elect shall become President. If a President shall not have been chosen before the time fixed for the beginning of his term, or if the President elect shall have failed to qualify, then the Vice President elect shall act as President until a President shall have qualified; and the Congress may by law provide for the case wherein neither a President elect nor a Vice President shall have qualified, declaring who shall then act as President, or the manner in which one who is to act shall be selected, and such person shall act accordingly until a President or Vice President shall have qualified.

Section IV

The Congress may by law provide for the case of the death of any of the persons from whom the House of Representatives may choose a President whenever the right of choice shall have devolved upon them, and for the case of the death of any of the persons from whom the Senate may choose a Vice President whenever the right of choice shall have devolved upon them.

Section V

Sections I and II shall take effect on the 15th day of October following the ratification of this article.

Section VI

This article shall be inoperative unless it shall have been ratified as an amendment to the Constitution by the legislatures of three-fourths of the several States within seven years from the date of its submission.

Amendment XXI

Section I

The eighteenth article of amendment to the Constitution of

the United States is hereby repealed.

Section II

The transportation or importation into any State, Territory, or Possession of the United States for delivery or use therein of intoxicating liquors, in violation of the laws thereof, is hereby prohibited.

Section III

This article shall be inoperative unless it shall have been ratified as an amendment to the Constitution by conventions in the several States, as provided in the Constitution, within seven years from the date of the submission hereof to the States by the Congress.

Amendment XXII

Section I

No person shall be elected to the office of the President more than twice, and no person who has held the office of President, or acted as President, for more than two years of a term to which some other person was elected President shall be elected to the office of President more than once. But this Article shall not apply to any person holding the office of President when this Article was proposed by Congress, and shall not prevent any person who may be holding the office of President, or acting as President, during the term within which this Article becomes operative from holding the office of President or acting as President during the remainder of such term.

Section II

This article shall be inoperative unless it shall have been ratified as an amendment to the Constitution by the legislatures of three-fourths of the several States within seven years from the date of its submission to the States by the Congress.

Amendment XXIII

Section I

The District constituting the seat of Government of the United States shall appoint in such manner as Congress may direct:

A number of electors of President and Vice President equal to the whole number of Senators and Representatives in Congress to which the District would be entitled if it were a State, but in no event more than the least populous State; they shall be in addition to those appointed by the States, but they shall be considered, for the purposes of the election of President and Vice President, to be electors appointed by a State; and they shall meet in the District and perform such duties as provided by the twelfth article of amendment.

Section II

The Congress shall have power to enforce this article by appropriate legislation.

Amendment XXIV

Section I

The right of citizens of the United States to vote in any primary or other election for President or Vice President, for electors for President or Vice President, or for Senator or Representative in Congress, shall not be denied or abridged by the United States or any State by reason of failure to pay any poll tax or other tax.

Section II

The Congress shall have power to enforce this article by appropriate legislation.

Amendment XXV

Section I

In case of the removal of the President from office or of his death or resignation, the Vice President shall become

President.

Section II

Whenever there is a vacancy in the office of the Vice President, the President shall nominate a Vice President who shall take office upon confirmation by a majority vote of both Houses of Congress.

Section III

Whenever the President transmits to the President pro tempore of the Senate and the Speaker of the House of Representatives his written declaration that he is unable to discharge the powers and duties of his office, and until he transmits to them a written declaration to the contrary, such powers and duties shall be discharged by the Vice President as Acting President.

Section IV

Whenever the Vice President and a majority of either the principal officers of the executive departments or of such other body as Congress may by law provide, transmit to the President pro tempore of the Senate and the Speaker of the House of Representatives their written declaration that the President is unable to discharge the powers and duties of his office, the Vice President shall immediately assume the powers and duties of the office as Acting President.

Thereafter, when the President transmits to the President pro tempore of the Senate and the Speaker of the House of Representatives his written declaration that no inability exists, he shall resume the powers and duties of his office unless the Vice President and a majority of either the principal officers of the executive department or of such other body as Congress may by law provide, transmit within four days to the President pro tempore of the Senate and the Speaker of the House of Representatives their written declaration that the President is unable to discharge the powers and duties of his office. Thereupon

Congress shall decide the issue, assembling within forty-eight hours for that purpose if not in session. If the Congress, within twenty-one days after receipt of the latter written declaration, or, if Congress is not in session, within twenty-one days after Congress is required to assemble, determines by two-thirds vote of both Houses that the President is unable to discharge the powers and duties of his office, the Vice President shall continue to discharge the same as Acting President; otherwise, the President shall resume the powers and duties of his office.

Amendment XXVI

Section I

The right of citizens of the United States, who are eighteen years of age or older, to vote shall not be denied or abridged by the United States or by any State on account of age.

Section II

The Congress shall have power to enforce this article by appropriate legislation.

Amendment XXVII

No law, varying the compensation for the services of the Senators and Representatives, shall take effect, until an election of representatives shall have intervened.

Appendix C

Modernized Text of the United States Constitution

Preamble

We the people of the United States deserve a more perfect Nation. In order achieve this goal we must establish Justice, insure domestic Peace, provide for the Nation's defense, and promote the general welfare. As part of this improved country we will secure the blessing of Independence. We must also guarantee these things for future generations. We will do these things in the newly formed United States of America.

Article I

Section I

All of the lawmaking powers allowed in this government are assigned to the Congress of the United States. The Congress will be broken down into two sections, or Houses, named the Senate and the House of Representatives.

Section II

The portion of the Congress known as the House of Representatives will be made up of membership with people chosen from every state in the Union. These members will be elected every two years.

In order to be a member of the United States House of Representatives (the lower house of Congress) an individual must be twenty-five years of age. The membership of this House must also have been a citizen of the United States for seven years and, when elected, live in the State he or she was elected to represent.

Representatives and taxes will be assigned to the States of the Union in proportion to their population.

The population of the States will be determined by adding up the number of free people, including those bound to service for some period of time. These populations will also exclude Indians, who will not be taxed, as well as three fifths of all other people (slaves).

The population of the States will be determined by conducting a census. The first census will be made within three years of the first meeting of the Congress of the United States and every ten years after that. This shall be done in a method that will be described by law.

The number of representatives that each state gets will not exceed one for every thirty thousand residents. Each State, regardless of population, will get at least one Representative.

Until a census can be achieved the State of New Hampshire will receive three, Massachusetts eight, Rhode Island and Providence Plantations one, Connecticut five, New York six, New Jersey four, Pennsylvania eight, Delaware one, Maryland six, Virginia ten, North Carolina five, South Carolina five and George three.

When a vacancy occurs (e.g. a representative resigns, is impeached or passes away) the Executive Authority (e.g. Governor) of the State who has lost a Representative shall issue a Writ of Election and fill the vacancy. This will cause a special election to be held, out of the normal election cycle, to allow the people of that State to choose a new Representative.

The House of Representatives will have the power to fill their leadership roles (e.g. Speaker of the House and other Officer positions). They shall also have the sole power of

Impeachment.

Section III

The Senate of the United States will be the Upper House of the Congress. This Legislative Body shall be made up of two Senators from each State. These Senators will not be chosen by the people but will be chosen by the Legislatures of each of the States. Each Senator will serve for a period of six years and get one vote.

Once the first Senate has been elected they will be divided into three equal groups. The seats of the first group will be vacated at the end of the second year, the second group will be vacated at the end of the fourth year, and the third group will be vacated at the end of the sixth year. As a result, one third of the Senate will be elected every second year. If vacancies occur as a result of resignation, or some other reason, while the Legislature of that State is on recess, the Executive of that State will fill those vacancies.

In order to serve as a Senator a person must be thirty-five years old, and have been a Citizen of the United States for at least nine years. They must also be a resident of the State they were elected to represent.

The Vice President of the United States is the President of the Senate. Despite this he does not vote on any legislation unless there is a tie amongst the Senators. In that instance it is the Vice President who casts the tie-breaking vote.

Other than the Vice President, the Senators shall choose their own officers, as well as a President pro tempore. The President pro tempore will be the person who acts in place of the Senate President when he is not available, for instance (but not limited to) when the Vice President had to take the office of President and no new Vice President has taken office.

The Senate is the only place where an impeachment trial

(e.g. punishment phase of the impeachment proceedings) will take place. When they meet for this purpose they shall do so only after taking an oath swearing to tell the truth. In the case of the impeachment of the President of the United States, the Chief Justice of the Supreme Court shall preside over the proceedings. No punishment from these trials shall be considered agreed upon unless two thirds of the Members vote yes.

In the case of an impeachment the punishment shall not be anything greater than removal from office, and disqualification to hold official office in the United States again. If a person is impeached they can be held liable for crimes committed and put on trial in a criminal court according to the law.

Section IV

The times, locations, and methods of holding elections for Senators and other Representatives will be determined by each of the States. However, Congress may, at any time, pass a law to alter the regulations put forward by the States with the exception of the location of the vote. The State can always determine the location of the vote.

Congress shall meet at least once every year. The first day of that meeting will be the first Monday in December unless a law has been passed that appoints a different day.

Section V

Each House in the Congress shall be able to determine if its members were justly elected and also be able to determine if they meet the Constitutional qualifications for the appropriate office.

In order to conduct business within either House a majority of members must be present and that majority will constitute what is called a Quorum. A number smaller than a quorum may adjourn from day to day, and that same smaller number is allowed to force additional members to attend in order to reach a quorum. If additional members refuse to attend, the two houses may impose whatever penalties they decide are appropriate.

The two Houses can write their own rules for their proceedings. They may also determine punishments for their own membership's disorderly behavior, should any occur. They may also, if two thirds of the membership agrees, expel, or dismiss a member.

Each House of Congress must keep notes of their proceedings. From time to time they must publish those notes, except for the portions they determine require secrecy, for example in the case of National Security. If one fifth of the members present agree, the voting record (yeas and nays) of the membership on any or all legislative votes should be part of those notes.

If Congress is in session neither House is allowed to adjourn without the consent of the other for more than three days. Additionally, neither house may meet at a location separate from the other.

Section VI

The Senators and Representatives will receive a salary for their services. The amount of that salary will be written into law and paid from the Treasury of the United States.

With the exception of treason, felony, and breach of peace members will not be arrested during their attendance at the meeting of their respective Houses. Members are not to be arrested for any reason, other than those listed, while traveling to and from those meetings for speeches or debates in either House. They are not to be questioned for crimes in any other place other than in their elected House.

No Senator or Representative, while serving in his or her elected office, shall be appointed to any civil office under the authority of the United States for which a salary is received. No person holding such a civil office, who is then elected to either the Senate or the House of Representatives, shall continue to hold that civil office while holding the elected office.

Section VII

All laws involving the collection of a tax shall start in the House of Representatives. The Senate may propose amendments in the same fashion they do on other Bills.

Every Bill that passes the House of Representatives and the Senate must be presented to the President of the United States. If the President approves of the Bill he can sign it, and then it is enacted into law. If he does not approve of it he can return it, with his objections to the House that originated it. The Legislature must enter the President's objections into their Journal and proceed to reconsider the Bill.

If, after reconsideration, two thirds of that House agrees to pass the Bill, it shall be sent along with the President's objections to the other House. If the other House passes it with two thirds of their members agreeing, it shall become law. In all such cases the votes of both Houses will be determined by voting yes or no and the Names of the representatives voting for and against the Bill will be entered into the Journal of the respective House.

If the President does not return a Bill within ten days (not counting Sundays) after it was presented to him or her, the Bill shall become a Law, just as if it had been signed. This time period is only effective in the cases when Congress is in session. If the Congress sends the President a Bill and within ten days adjourns to prevent the Bill's return, the Bill will not become law.

Every order, resolution or vote that the Senate and House of Representatives agree upon (except the motion to adjourn) shall be presented to the President of the United

States. Before that order, resolution, or vote can take effect it shall be approved or disapproved by the President. If it is disapproved by the President it will only be enacted after it passes by the two thirds majority of the Senate and House of Representatives according to the rules and limitations prescribed in this section of the Constitution.

Section VIII

The Congress has the power to enact and collect taxes, duties, or excises. This is done in order to pay debts, provide for the common defense, as well as the general welfare of the United States. All of these Federal taxes, duties and excises must be uniform throughout the United States.

The Congress has the power to borrow money using the credit of the United States.

The Congress has the power to regulate commerce with foreign Nations, among the States as well as with the Indian Tribes.

The Congress has the power to establish a uniform Rule of Naturalization, and uniform laws on the subject of Bankruptcies throughout the United States.

The Congress has the power to coin money, as well as regulate its value. They are also to fix the standard of weights and measures of that money.

The Congress has the power to pass punishments for the counterfeiting of Securities and current Coin of the United States.

The Congress has the power to establish a post office and post roads.

The Congress has the power to promote the progress of Science and useful Arts. This is done by securing, for limited times, the rights to authors and inventors the rights to their writings and discoveries in the form of copyrights and patents.

The Congress has the power to confirm judges in Courts lower than the Supreme Court.

The Congress has the power to punish piracies and felonies committed on the high Seas as well as offenses against the Law of Nations.

The Congress has the power to declare War, grant letters of retaliation against an enemy and to make rules concerning the capture of enemy combatants upon the land and water during times of conflict.

The Congress has the power to raise and support Armies, however, no appropriation of money for this use will be valid for more than two years.

The Congress has the power to build and maintain a Navy.

The Congress has the power to make rules for the governance and regulations of the Land and Naval Armed Forces.

The Congress has the power to provide for calling up the militia to execute the Laws of the Union, as well as to suppress revolt and repel an invasion.

The Congress has the power to provide for the organization, arming and disciplining of the militia as well as governing that part of the militia that is employed in the service of the Federal Government of the United States of America. The Congress shall reserve to the States the appointment of Officers and the authority to train the militia according to the discipline put forward by the Congress.

The Congress has the power to exercise exclusive legislation in all cases over the Nation's Capital. This power to exclusive legislation also pertains to all lands purchased by the consent of legislature for the building of forts, magazines, arsenals, dockyards and other needed federal buildings.

The Congress has the power to make all the laws necessary and proper for carrying into execution the powers listed in, and all other powers entrusted by this Constitution in the Government of the United States or any Department or Office it enacts into existence.

Section IX

The immigration of people coming into the United States shall not be prohibited by the Congress prior to the year one thousand eight hundred and eight; however Congress may decide to collect a tax on immigrants during that time, not to exceed ten dollars per person.

The right of a citizen to appear before a judge shall not be suspended, except in the case of rebellion or invasion when the public safety may require otherwise.

A law passed after a citizen has performed an act that would break that new law has no relevance to the act committed.

No tax can be charged for the right to vote.

No tax can be charged on goods or services exported from one State and imported to another.

No regulation of commerce shall be passed that gives preference to a port of one State over another. Transportation bound to one state shall not be obligated to pay taxes upon entrance to another state.

No money shall be taken from the Treasury of the United States except when a law is passed directing the expenditure. A regular statement and accounting of the receipts and expenditures of all public money shall be published from time to time.

No title of Nobility will be granted by the United States.

No person holding any office that is salaried by the government will take a gift, office, or title from a king, prince or foreign state without the permission of Congress.

Section X

No State can enter into a treaty, alliance or Confederation.

No State may grant letters of retaliation against an enemy.

No State shall coin money.

No State shall make anything but gold and silver coin money for payment of debts.

No State shall pass a Bill that infringes on a person's civil rights.

No State shall pass a law that causes infractions of the past to be in violation of that law.

No State shall pass a law imparting the obligation of contracts or grant the Title of Nobility to any person.

No State shall, without the consent of the Congress, tax any imports or exports, except what may be absolutely necessary for executing its inspection laws.

The net product of taxes by any State on imports or exports shall be for the use of the Treasury of the United States; and all such laws shall be subject to the revision as well as control of the Congress.

No State shall, without the consent of Congress, engage in War with another State or foreign power unless actually invaded or under such imminent danger that delay would cause harm to their citizens.

Article II

Section I

Executive authority will be given to the President and Vice President of the United States of America. They will have a term of four years and will be selected at the same time.

Their election will occur in the following fashion:

Each of the states will choose, in any way the law sees fit, a number of electors equal to the number of Representatives and Senators each State has in the Congress. A Senator, Representative or anyone holding a position of power and authority in the United States Government cannot be selected as an Elector.

Each Elector will meet in their state and vote for two people by ballot. One of those two people cannot reside in their own state. The electors will make a list of all people voted for and the number of votes received, then send the results in a sealed manner with the transcription signed and certified with the names of each elector and vote tallies to the President of the Senate.

The President of the Senate will open each transcription in front of the Senate and count each person and the number of votes. The person with the highest votes becomes the President of the United States. If there is not a majority winner, or a tie, the House of Representatives will choose a winner. The person with the second highest votes becomes the Vice President of the United States.

The body of Congress will set a date and a time for the Electors to place their votes. This date and time will be the same across the entire United States.

Only a person who is born a citizen of the United States or has become a Naturalized Citizen of the United States at the time this document is accepted can become the President. Anyone who would become the President would have to be at least thirty five years old and have been a resident of the United States for the previous fourteen years.

If the office of the President is vacated due to death, mental illness, resignation, or legal removal, the Vice President shall take over the authority of the Presidency.

Congress may, if the situation demands it, name a person to stand as President until either a new President is elected or the current President has overcome his disability.

The President and Vice President will receive a salary for their service. This salary will be the same amount the entire time they served as the President or Vice President. They will not receive any other payment from the government.

Before the newly elected President takes his place in office, he must swear an oath stating that he will "Faithfully execute the duties of the Office of the President of the United States to the best of his ability and protect and defend the Constitution of the United States."

Section II

The President is the overall Commander of all the military forces of the United States as well as the State Militias when the situation requires.

Reprieves, as well as pardons, can be granted by the President for any offence against the United States expect in cases of impeachment.

With advice and approval of the Senate, the President can make treaties with other countries, provided that two thirds of the Senate agrees. He shall also appoint Ambassadors, public ministers, Judges of the Supreme Court and other positions that appointments are not provided for, but are created by law. Congress must, by law, confirm all appointments of lower officers, courts of law or Department heads. In the event of a person not being confirmed, the President must supply a new candidate.

The President can fill any vacant position during a recess of the Senate by granting a commission that will expire at the end of the new session. These will be referred to as recess appointments.

Section III

Once a year, the President will address the full Congress and present the State of the Union, and relate a future vision and direction for the United States. He can address one or both Houses during extraordinary circumstances and will mediate between the House of Representatives and the Senate if they do not agree.

Section IV

The President, Vice President and all civilian officers of the United States will be removed from office for treason, bribery, or serious crimes or misdemeanors.

Article III

Section I

The Judicial Power of the United States shall reside in one Supreme Court as well as any inferior courts that the Congress may establish. The Judges at the Supreme Court and lower courts shall hold their offices during times of good behavior, for life, without the need of reappointment. The judges of all courts shall receive compensation for their service, which cannot be lowered at any point during their time in office.

Section II

The power of the Judicial Branch shall apply to all cases both in Law and in Equity that apply under this Constitution, the Laws of the United States, and treaties that shall be made under their authority.

The power of the Judicial Branch shall apply to all cases affecting Ambassadors, or other public officials whose office is meant to look after the commercial interests of the citizenry while in other countries.

The power of the Judicial Branch shall apply to all cases of maritime jurisdiction.

The power of the Judicial Branch shall be to decide controversies to which the United States is a party. These include controversies between two or more States, between a State and citizens of another State, between citizens of different States, between citizens of the same State claiming lands under grants of different States, and between a State or the citizens of a State and foreign states citizens or subjects.

The Supreme Court has jurisdiction over all cases affecting Ambassadors, other public caretakers such as Consuls, and those in which one of the States is a Party to the action. The Supreme Court shall be the court of final appeal, there is no higher court and their decisions are the final decision on any matter brought before them for decision. The only recourse after their decision is to petition Congress to change the law.

The trial of all crimes, with the exception of Impeachment, shall be by Jury. The trial for any crime will be held in the State where it was committed. If a crime was not committed within any State the trial shall be at a place or places that the Congress has directed by Law.

Section III

Treason against the United States will be defined as levying War against them by being devoted to an enemy, or by giving an enemy aid and comfort. No person will be convicted of Treason unless there is testimony of two witnesses to the same overt Act or, upon their Confession in open Court.

The Congress has the power to declare the punishment for Treason. No one guilty of treason shall be punished except during the life of the person. Their ancestors cannot be held to account for their crime(s).

Article IV

Section I

Full confidence and trust will be given to each State in the area of public actions, record keeping and legal procedures by every other State. The Congress may decide how those beliefs and trusts will be proven and their results.

Section II

Everyone will have the same identical, and indistinguishable rights and privileges in each and every State of the Union.

A person, who has been found guilty of a felony, treason or other crime and escapes from justice of one State but is caught in another, will be sent back to the State from which the person escaped upon request of the Executive leadership of the original State.

A person held to service or labor in one State, under the Laws of the State, who escapes into another, shall not be discharged from such service or labor, but shall be delivered up upon a claim by the party to whom such service or labor is due.

Section III

Congress can allow the admittance of new States into the United States. No State or States can be made within or from another State or merge two or more States or sections of States without the agreement of both State governances and the Congress.

Congress has the power to make rules and guidelines concerning territories and lands belonging to the government of the United States. This Constitution should not be used to change any claim of the United States or any specific State.

Section IV

The Federal Government will let the States elect their own government and will protect each State from hostile takeover by another State.

Article V

Amendments to this Constitution can be made when either the Congress by two thirds majority of both houses deem it necessary or when the Legislatures of two thirds majority of the several States call for a Convention for proposing Amendments. In either case, these amendments will be considered as part of this Constitution when ratified by the Legislatures of three fourth of the States.

No amendment may be made prior to the year one thousand eight hundred and eight that shall affect the first and fourth clauses in the ninth section of the first article. No State, without its consent, shall be deprived of its equal voting rights in the Senate.

Article VI

All debts incurred or obligations entered into, before the adoption of this Constitution, shall be considered valid debts or agreements with the United States of America under the Constitution, just as they were under the Articles of Confederation.

This Constitution, and the laws of the United States made as a result of it, and all treaties made under the authority of the United States are the supreme law of the land. The judges in every State shall be bound by these laws, in spite of the laws of any State to the contrary.

The Senators, Representatives, Members of the several State Legislatures, and all Executive as well as Judicial Officers of both the United States and the several States shall swear an Oath to support this Constitution. No religious test shall ever be required as a qualification to any office or public trust under the United States.

Article VII

This ratification of the convention of nine States shall be sufficient to establish this Constitution between the States.

This was done in convention by the unanimous consent of the States present on the seventeenth day of September in the year of our Lord one thousand seven hundred and eighty seven. We have voted on this Constitution and inscribed our names,

Amendment I

Congress will not pass any law that establishes a national religion or prohibiting someone from practicing any religion.

Congress will not pass any law preventing the freedoms of speech or of the press. Citizens should be free to say or publish anything they see fit. Other citizens are free to read or not read anything they see fit.

Congress will not pass any law preventing the citizenry to peacefully assemble.

Congress will not pass any law preventing the citizenry from petitioning their Government for changes to a policy or law that may be unfairly treating the citizens of The United States of America.

Amendment II

A well maintained, and regulated civilian armed Paramilitary (Militia) is needed to provide security to the country. The people have a right to own and keep firearms and this right will not be taken away or lessened.

Amendment III

Soldiers cannot take over a privately owned home or stay in a privately owned home unless the owner agrees, without duress, either in peacetime or during armed conflict.

Soldiers must act within all accordances of the laws of

personal ownership.

Amendment IV

Law enforcement shall not, without having a specified reason, search or seize any personal items of a citizen. Probable cause has to be stated clearly and in detail describe what is being searched for and where these things are being searched for, and it must be taken to the legal authority before any search and seizure can be done and a warrant issued. Every reasonable effort must be taken to explain the purpose of the search and seizure prior to it taking place.

Amendment V

No one will be held for a crime unless so ordered by a grand jury or judge. The exception is the military forces during times of war or public danger. The military can also issue this order in those times mentioned.

A person shall *not* be tried for the same crime twice or be a witness against their own persons.

No one will have their life, liberty or property taken from them without legal judgment or have their personal belongs taken for public use without payment for those belongings.

Amendment VI

In all criminal matters, a person has the right to a fair and impartial trial within the State and District of the alleged crime.

Each person shall be informed of the nature of the crime for which they are accused and have witness presented both for, and against the person in question, and the accused will have the right to legal counsel for their defense.

Amendment VII

In lawsuits with a value of more than twenty dollars, a person has a right to a trial by jury. No case tried by a jury shall be tried a second time.

Amendment VIII

Incredibly high bails, fines or cruel and unusual punishments will not be used against a citizen.

Amendment IX

The enumeration in the Constitution of very specific rights shall not be used to deny or denigrate other rights retained by the people.

Amendment X

The powers not given to the Federal Government by the Constitution, or not prohibited by it, are powers for the States or the people themselves.

Amendment XI

Legal power of the Federal Government won't be changed or extended to any other legal matter already ongoing against a person of any State by another State or citizen of a different country.

Amendment XII

Each elector will vote within their own State for two people, one of which is not of their own State to become the President of the United States. They shall do this in writing.

Those ballots are then sent to the President of Congress to be tallied and recorded. The person with the most tallies becomes the President of the United States. The person with the second largest amount of tallies becomes the Vice President of the United States.

If there is no majority vote for the President, the House of Representatives will immediately choose the President. But those votes will be done by State (each state getting 1 vote).

If there is no majority for the office of Vice President, the Senate will take the top two names and select a Vice president by a two-thirds vote.

If there is no selection for the President by the Fourth of March, then the vice president will hold the office of President until one is elected.

If a person is ineligible to be the President of the United States, then that person cannot be the Vice President of the United States.

Amendment XIII

Section I

Slavery or involuntary servitude will be illegal in the United States except in matters of punishment for a committed crime inside the United States or its territories.

Section II

Congress will enforce this law with appropriate legislation.

Amendment XIV

Section I

All citizens of the United States either born or naturalized are subject to the laws of the United States and the States in which they live. States may not make laws which remove from the citizens their rights and privileges of being a Citizen. No States will confine a person without legal due process nor deny anyone the right to due process under the law.

Section II

The number of representatives in each state is selected by the number of voting males over the age of 21 years and citizens, but not involved in armed rebellion against the government of the United States or guilty of other crimes against federal laws. The number of males will be reduced by the number of representatives in proportion over the age of 21 years that have lost the right to vote.

Section III

No person shall hold elected office in either State or Federal government who has taken up arms or insurrection against the federal government of the United States. Congress with a two-thirds vote from each house can remove this restriction from an individual.

Section IV

The United States government will not question the responsibility of public debt obtained as payment of military pensions or bounties in service in suppression of armed revolt.

The United States will not take on the debt of those who were in armed revolt against the United States. All claims of loss of income, debt, or loss of property and all obligations will be held as illegal and not the responsibility of the government of the United States.

Section V

Congress and the federal government will enforce this amendment to the Constitution.

Amendment XV

Section I

The right to vote will not be denied due to race, color, or having previously been a slave.

Section II

Congress and the Federal government will enforce this amendment to the Constitution.

Amendment XVI

Congress can levy taxes on income regardless of type of income, without regard to the size of each State.

Amendment XVII

The Senate of the United States has two members from each state. The citizens of that State elect these Senators from their own State. Each term will be only six years and each Senator will get one vote. The State government will set the requirements for election of Senator.

If a Senate seat becomes open, the State executive (the Governor) can create an election to fill the opening provided the State Legislature has not granted the Governor the ability to make a temporary selection until a vote can take place to elect a new Senator.

This amendment will not affect any ongoing elections or terms of current Senator chosen before accepted as part of the Constitution.

Amendment XVIII

Section I

One year from the date of accepting this Amendment as part of the Constitution, the making, distilling, transporting, selling or consuming alcoholic beverages, bringing in, importing alcohol or exporting alcohol to or from the United States or its territories is illegal.

Section II

Congress and State Government will both have the power to enforce this law.

Section III

This amendment will not go into affect unless Congress has accepted it as part of the Constitution within seven years from the date of submission.

Amendment XIX

The right to vote as a citizen of the United States will not be denied or changed by the United States or any state on account of what gender the citizen.

Congress shall enforce this law.

Amendment XX

Section I

The newly elected President and Vice President shall take office on January 20th and the members of Congress will begin their terms on January 3rd on the year their terms are to begin.

Section II

Congress will meet at 12 Noon on January 3rd of each year unless the date is changed by law.

Section III

The Vice President-elect shall act as President if the President-elect dies before he or she can take office, is found to be unqualified, or unable to hold the office of President. By law Congress can declare a situation where both the President and Vice President elect are unfit, unqualified or unable to hold their offices. Congress will then select a person to act as President until a new President can be qualified.

Section IV

If there is a case of a death of the President and Vice President at the same period of time, the Congress has the right to select a President by the House of Representatives and a Vice President by the Senate.

Section V

Sections I and II shall take effect on the 15th of October following the ratification of this article.

Section VI

This article shall be inoperative unless it shall have been ratified as an amendment to the Constitution by the legislatures of three-fourths of the several States within seven years from the date of its submission.

Amendment XXI

Section I

The 18th amendment to the Constitution is removed or invalidated.

Section II

Transporting or importing alcohol into any State or Territory of the United States in which a local government has created a law against alcohol, is still illegal.

Section III

This article will be not be used unless accepted as part of the Constitution within seven years of the date it was submitted to congress.

Amendment XXII

Section I

No person can hold the office of President more than twice.

No person who has be in office as President for more than two years of a term of another elected President can hold the elected office of President more than once.

This amendment will not affect any standing person holding the office of President or acting as the office of President during the remainder of their term.

Section II

This will not go into affect unless accepted by three-fourths vote of congress within seven years from the date of submission.

Amendment XXIII

Section I

Congress decides where the capital (The District of Columbia) of the United States will be.

The District of Columbia will be granted the same number of electors as the least populace state within the United States for the purpose of voting for the office of President and Vice President.

Those electors shall meet in the District and do their job as stated in the Twelfth Amendment.

Section II

Congress will enforce this law.

Amendment XXIV

Section I

There will be no fee, cost or tax for the right to vote as a citizen in an election of the United States for the office or President, Vice President, or members of both houses of Congress.

Section II

Congress will enforce this law.

Amendment XXV

Section I

The Vice President will become President if the current President dies in office, resigns or is impeached and removed.

Section II

In the event of a vacancy the President can select a new Vice President who, on a majority vote from both houses of Congress, takes that office.

Section III

When the sitting President has sent to the leaders of both houses of Congress his or her written declaration that he or she is unable to act as President, the Vice President shall take over the duties of the office of President until the President sends a written letter to the leaders of Congress declaring his renewed ability to be the President.

Section IV

When the Vice President and other Leaders of the Executive departments can, by law, send their written declaration of the unfitness of the standing President. The Vice President shall take over the duties as acting President.

If and when the President sends the leaders of Congress his/her written statement that no inability exists, they resume the powers and duties of President, unless the Vice President and the other leaders of the Executive Departments send within four days their statement of the Presidents inability or discharge the duties and responsibilities of his office. Congress at this time will decide the issue, assembling within forty-eight hours for this purpose, if not in session. If Congress, within twenty-one days determines by a two-thirds majority vote of both houses the Presidents inability to perform their duties, the Vice President will continue on as Acting President. Otherwise, the President will once again take over the duties and responsibilities of his or her office.

Amendment XXVI

Section I

Citizens of the United States who are eighteen years of age or older have the right to vote

Section II

Congress will enforce this law.

Amendment XXVII

No pay raise for Senators and Representatives will take effect until the current term of office has ended.

Appendix D
Author Biographies

Timothy Imholt PhD

I was an enlisted soldier in the Army who was honorably discharged in 1996. After receiving my discharge at the age of 24, I attended the University of North Texas where I earned a B.S. and Ph.D. in Physics all on my own dime.

Upon graduation, I took a job working for a startup company researching and developing nanotechnologies for use in alternative energies before accepting a position at the Raytheon Corporation. During my time at Raytheon, I have worked on a variety of advanced technologies and am credited as either the sole or the co-inventor on 14 United States Patents. Throughout my career, I have written or co-authored a variety of scientific papers discussing everything from the environment and behavior of global temperature cycles to topics regarding various uses for nanotechnology based structures in alternative fuels and even a few on new lightweight armor systems for our soldiers.

In addition to my work in fundamental and applied science, I have written two fictional novels titled Nuclear Assault, and The Forest of Assassins. The main premise of the former was to show what could happen if a rogue nation had functional nuclear weaponry and a willingness to use them. The latter is a combination of true accounts and fiction, set in the Vietnam War.

I am a family man married to my lovely wife Jean. Together we are raising our three children, two small boys and baby girl. I also have an older daughter from a previous marriage who is currently attending college in Texas.

Our oldest boy (Elliot) turned four years old recently and is very proud of now being fully potty trained as well as reaching the milestone of going to pre-school. He holds the record as the sweetest boy in his preschool for bringing tissues to kids who cry almost every time.

The younger boy (Emmit) is two and a half and enjoys playing with Elliot and stealing his younger sister's snack off her high chair. He has been a little bit late in developing his speech but lately has flourished through early intervention services and now starting to communicate with people.

The youngest child (Erin) was welcomed to the world in January 2013 and is currently learning to play with her brothers. She may turn out to be the one that runs the house as both of the boys have figured out that when she wants something, you'd better let her have it.

My wife is Jiyun (Jean) Imholt was born in Seoul, South Korea. Jean immigrated to the United States at fifteen years old with her parents. Before immigrating, Jean's father was an athletics coach earning the honor of coaching the 1984 South Korean Women's Olympic rowing team while her mother was a teacher before coming to the United States.

Michael Garst

Michael was born in 1972 in the great state of Texas and grew up reading science fiction of all types.

After high school, he joined the U.S. Army and severed proudly until 2000 when he was honorably discharged.

Currently, he lives in the people's democratic state of Wisconsin with a very understanding wife, two lazy dogs and two wonderful high-energy kids.

Michael has earned a B.S. in Management from Cardinal Strictch University. This is Michaels debut work on a book, but will not be his last.

www.ingramcontent.com/pod-product-compliance
Lightning Source LLC
Chambersburg PA
CBHW030434290526
45786CB00001B/280